THE GOLDEN AGE of JAZZ

THE GOLDEN AGE of JAZZ

Text and Photographs by

William P. Gottlieb

POMEGRANATE ARTBOOKS • SAN FRANCISCO

This book is dedicated to Walter Schaap and to his son, Phil, who, each in his own way, have done so much to strengthen the beat of jazz.

Published 1995 by Pomegranate Communications, Inc.

Box 6099, Rohnert Park, California 94927

© 1979 William P. Gottlieb

This Pomegranate Artbooks edition of *The Golden Age of Jazz* is a revised and expanded version of the first edition published by Simon & Schuster in 1979. It is published by arrangement with the author.

The photographs in this book are in the Gottlieb Collection of the Library of Congress (Ira and Leonore S. Gershwin Fund).

Visit www.jazzphotos.com, then click on the Library of Congress link for more photographs and text. Or go directly to http://memory.loc.gov/ammem/wghtml/wghome.html

William Gottlieb took the photographs in this book between 1939 and 1948. They were made with a Speed Graphic, a Graflex, and a Rolleiflex; the principal source of artificial light was flashbulbs.

Library of Congress Cataloging-in-Publication Data

Gottlieb, William P.
    The golden age of jazz / by William P. Gottlieb. — 1st ed.
        p.   cm.
    Reprint. Originally published: New York : Simon and Schuster, 1979.
    ISBN 0-87654-355-7 (pbk.)
    1. Jazz musicians—Portraits. 2. Jazz—pictorial works.
ML3506.G68   1995
781.65'09—dc20   94-49640
                                     CIP
                                     MN

Designed by Bonnie Smetts Design

09 08 07 06 05 04 03 02 01
13 12 11 10 9 8 7 6 5 4

PRINTED IN KOREA

CONTENTS

FOREWORD

If one could pick a time in which to live for the sake of jazz, it would almost have to be the decade in which Bill Gottlieb worked as a writer-photographer, from 1938 to 1948. Most of the musicians who had established the style of early jazz in New Orleans and recorded the masterpieces that are its enduring monuments were not only alive but still active, as were the leaders of the swing era, from Kansas City and Chicago to New York, together with younger musicians who were creating bebop on New York's legendary 52nd Street during its brief period as the center for one of the most exciting developments in the history of American music. No wonder this time has been called the Golden Age of Jazz.

Melodic improvisers Louis Armstrong, Lester Young, and Charlie Parker; composers Duke Ellington and Thelonious Monk; pianists Willie "the Lion" Smith, Art Tatum, and Nat "King" Cole; vocalists Billie Holiday, Ella Fitzgerald, and Frank Sinatra; these are among the many subjects of Gottlieb's brilliant and incisive portraits, and, in their wide diversity, they remind us of how rich that era was in originality and individualism—all thriving in the commercial milieu of American popular music. There is that anomalous giant (musically speaking) "Leadbelly," the blues singer and ex-convict, here contrived by Gottlieb's low angle and hard lighting to meet popular expectations of a menacing figure; Count Basie, the great leader of the swing era, a serene and reassuring pres-

ence in an often tumultuous profession, smiling from the keyboard at an unseen audience; Dizzy Gillespie, a publicist's dream, who probably understood the business of music better than any other jazzman then, in a clownish pose under a lamppost on 52nd Street; an intriguing study of a dance-hall audience surrounding regally seated Kenton band singer June Christy; and a spellbound Miles Davis gazing up in total concentration at the older, well-established bop trumpeter Howard McGhee. These are among the sometimes poignant, sometimes amusing, yet always illuminating images of Gottlieb's work with the stars of jazz's most prolific era.

Gottlieb wrote about them, first as a jazz columnist for the *Washington Post,* later for *Down Beat* magazine, among others. And when his employers would not provide a photographer to follow him on assignments, he bought a press camera and, through his own efforts (and at his own expense) became a portrait photographer of the first rank. As spontaneous as many of these pictures seem, they are not candid shots, nor are they culled from dozens of trials. Because film, and especially flashbulbs, were expensive and bulky, three or four exposures per session—all made "on location"—were the rule. Therefore, considerable thought went into the preparation of each picture. It is indeed fortuitous that Gottlieb's natural photographic genius emerged from his need to illustrate his writings during jazz's Golden Age. The result is his now widely acclaimed artistic legacy, which, more

than a mere documentary record, is itself one of the monuments of that age.

Exhibitions of Gottlieb's work have appeared in nearly one hundred institutions throughout the world, from the Navio Museum in Osaka, Japan, to the Museum of Modern Art in Stockholm, Sweden. His photographs have appeared in books, magazines, and newspapers, as well as on posters, postcards, T-shirts, and even drinking mugs. And they have been the acknowledged basis for four portraits of jazz musicians appearing on U.S. commemorative postage stamps. It is with pride that, through the generosity of the Ira and Lenore S. Gershwin Fund, the Library of Congress now counts the original negatives of Gottlieb's jazz photographs among its treasures, to be preserved permanently and made available for research.

The publication of this book, which coincides with the Library's acquisition of Gottlieb's work, is the first edition in high-quality duotone reproductions of his collection that originally appeared under the title *The Golden Age of Jazz.* It is, therefore, the first extensive publication of Gottlieb's pictures that does justice to the quality of the originals.

—*James H. Billington,*
The Librarian of Congress

PREFACE

My interest in jazz had its origins in a piece of improperly cooked pork. This malevolent tidbit was served at my Lehigh University fraternity house in 1936, just a day before the end of my sophomore year. When I arrived home for summer vacation, I promptly succumbed to trichinosis, a sometimes fatal but always uncomfortable disorder.

During convalescence, my most frequent visitor was "Doc" Bartle, a friend from high school days and, oddly, the son of the village blacksmith. Doc was an amateur classical pianist of little merit; however, he was an erudite scholar who subscribed to a couple of European music magazines, from which he learned that jazz was America's most original contribution to the arts. Doc couldn't get the hang of playing it, but he became an ardent fan and a collector of jazz records, which he constantly played for bedridden me, whether I liked it or not. I was a captive audience. Before long, I acquired Doc's love of jazz. By the time my health permitted me to shift from horizontal to vertical, I was hooked. Ellington and Armstrong joined my pantheon of heroes, right alongside Bach and Mozart.

Back at school, as editor of the campus monthly magazine, *The Lehigh Review,* I managed to devote at least one piece each issue to the glories of jazz. This was also the time when aspiring journalists had their eyes on *Life* magazine, with its spectacular photography. So I loaded the *Review* with pictures, using the camera talents of other

students (one of whom, Lou Stoumen, years later won two Academy Awards for short subjects he produced and photographed).

Upon graduation in 1938, with the Great Depression still depressed, I was fortunate to land a job, at $25 a week, in the advertising department of the *Washington Post.* Prompted by an urge to write, to make more money, and to spread the gospel, I persuaded the *Post's* managing editor to let me have a weekly jazz column (possibly the world's first regular jazz feature in a major newspaper). That added another $10 to my weekly pay.

I then convinced the editor to assign a photographer when I covered musical events. But after a few weeks, the editor called a halt: "Listen, kid, it's too expensive." But I was determined to have photo illustrations. At my own expense, I bought a Speed Graphic—the bulky and complex camera that newspaper staffers used. After making every mistake possible, I mastered the beast and became thenceforth a writer-photographer, though I was paid only for the writing, not the photography.

Once the column was established, I parlayed it into a weekly radio show on WRC/NBC and a three-a-week on a local station, WINX. By age twenty-two, I'd become Washington's "Mr. Jazz."

The *Post's* fiscal restraint in denying me the use of a photographer was a blessing. Becoming my own camera-man not only enhanced my column but eventually led to my becoming a

photo officer in the Air Corps during World War II and, still later, helped me become a staff writer for *Down Beat* magazine, a job I clinched because I could illustrate my own articles (though, again, I was paid only for the writing).

I stayed with jazz until 1948, then quit cold turkey to become a producer of educational filmstrips. As such, I released 1,400 titles and personally wrote about 400 of them. I also published nearly 20,000 photographs—none related to jazz. After retiring in 1979, by which time I had become president of a division of McGraw-Hill, I wrote some books, including *The Golden Age of Jazz,* which utilizes some 200 of my pre-1949 photographs.

With few exceptions, my jazz photographs, all taken on location instead of in studios, were made only to illustrate my articles. This supplemental function profoundly influenced my style: I consciously tried to take pictures that would augment my text, that would say something that would go beyond what I could do with just words. Ideally, I tried to capture a subject's personality or inner qualities. I reached these elusive goals only occasionally, though sometimes very successfully, as with the shot of Billie Holiday that clearly shows the anguish in her voice. At the very least, I tried to say *something* visually significant. When photographing Django Reinhardt, for example, the Belgian Gypsy who revolutionized guitar playing despite a fingering hand that was mutilated in his youth when his Gypsy caravan burned down, I made sure the viewer could see the inoperative fingers.

Other influences on my style were the facts that I wasn't paid for my photographs; that I used bulky, expensive cameras, film, and flashbulbs; and that taking pictures was not my primary objective. For those reasons, I made few exposures, typically two or three of an evening. As a result, I learned to shoot very carefully. I knew the music, I knew the musicians, I knew in advance when the right moment would arrive. It was *purposeful* shooting.

Finally, I was influenced by the knowledge that my pictures would be at the mercy of a newspaper or magazine layout person. Would I be given one column for a shot, or two, or more? If I photographed a group of ten musicians (which would have to be done horizontally), and if the resulting picture were then compressed into a single column, or even two, each musician would end up a pinhead. So I usually had only one or two musicians in a picture and got in close. Also, I mostly shot verticals. One musician. Close up. Vertical. Even if the picture were confined to a single column, it would still be meaningful to the viewer.

Well, that's about it. This kind of shooting, as well as being in the right place at the right time, has permitted me to have an eminently fruitful postretirement career. I sometimes wonder what I'd be doing now if it weren't for a serendipitous piece of badly cooked pork.

—*William P. Gottlieb*

AN APPRECIATION

For me, to open this book and view Bill Gottlieb's photographs of the New York jazz scene in the mid '40s is to revisit some of the most delightful experiences of my teen years. I have adored jazz ever since at age seven I first heard Sidney Bechet on radio. Besides the radio record shows, I could go to the Commodore Record Shop on 42nd & Lex to preview the latest releases in one of their listening booths. Until age fifteen, the only live performances I attended were the big-band stage shows at the RKO Boston and New York's midtown Paramount, Strand, Capital, and Roxy Theaters. However, on one Friday evening, feeling an extra flow of chutzpah, my buddies and I squeezed up to the bar at the 3 Deuces on 52nd Street and ordered Cokes for seventy-five cents each. To our utmost joy, we were served rather than shown the door because of our youth. So started my nights on The Street, and later, when strippers replaced the jazz, on Broadway at the Royal Roost, Bop City, and Birdland.

This was such a very special time for the music. Jazz was undergoing revolutionary changes, and the 52nd Street clubs, along with Minton's and Small's in Harlem, were the on-the-job experimental workshops. Gottlieb's images are a remarkable, intimate documentation of the period—in particular, the shot of Bird with his new protégé Red Rodney listening to Dizzy. Red recalled in an interview with pianist-writer Ben Sidran that when Bird wanted to hire him, he protested that he wasn't ready yet, that

Bird should go for Fats Navarro or Kenny Dorham. Bird persisted, however, saying that he knew a good player when he heard one. A bit later, Bird showed the same confidence in a neophyte named Miles Davis, and we have Bill's picture of the two of them playing together. There are classic shots of "the president of the tenor saxophone," Lester Young, with the horn at his trademark tilt, along with a picture of Allen Eager, one of the first stylistic offspring of Pres, with his tenor at a similar angle. Bill got many images of Dizzy. One that is rather humorous is with Ella around the time he taught her how to scat. If I were to choose my favorite photograph in the collection, it would be the one of a happy Davey Tough. A somewhat tragic figure, often in the shadow of showmen drummers Krupa and Rich, Davey's driving presence in the bands of Goodman, Shaw, Dorsey, and Woody Herman's First Herd always brought them to their peak performances.

The other experimental workshops were in the established big bands of Ellington, Basie, Hines, Barnet, Herman, Thornhill, and Kenton, as well as in those that appeared and disappeared in a flash: Georgie Auld's with Tiny Kahn, Red Rodney, Sonny Berman, and Serge Chaloff; Billy Eckstine's with Fats Navarro, Dexter Gordon, Gene Ammons, Art Blakey, Bird, and Diz; and Boyd Raeburn's with Lucky Thompson, Conti Candoli, Buddy DeFranco, and the ubiquitous Dizzy. Raeburn was one of the first to record Dizzy's "A Night in Tunisia," doing so

under its original title, "Interlude."

What a triumph of Bill's photographic skill, as well as his diplomacy, to be able to retain the mood and intimacy of the scene while using such cumbersome equipment. He was one of the last jazz photographers to use a large-format camera, flashbulbs or lights, and sheet film in this context. (Others included Herman Leonard and *Life* magazine's Chuck Peterson and Gjon Mili.) The 35mm camera/fast lens/fast film/forced film development photography revolution peaked in the late '40s, and those of us who became involved during those years, driven by an appreciation of our pioneering predecessors, had a somewhat easier time of it.

Bill and I did not meet until a few years ago, when I began to use his prints in the exhibits I curate under the title "The Jazz Image." However, his work, which appeared regularly in *Down Beat* in the '40s, had quite an influence on me even before I picked up a camera. I was sketching and painting at the time and used several of his pictures as models. My first Manhattan art exhibit was of these drawings at the public library branch on East 29th Street at Second Avenue in 1947. Bill stopped photographing jazz in 1948, just as I was beginning. He spent the next thirty-four years in the educational book and film field and then retired in 1979. At that point, he brought the old negatives and prints out of storage and began putting his treasure trove of material back into circulation. *The Golden Age of Jazz* was printed and reprinted several times prior to the production of this edition. Because of the recent advances in printing technology, this edition boasts reproduction quality approaching that of his original prints. Bill's collection of prints has been on the road, traveling to many galleries and museums throughout the United States, the Far East, and Europe, and quite a few prints have entered the private collections of jazz lovers. Not long ago, one photograph of Duke Ellington was acquired by the National Portrait Gallery, and now Bill's entire body of work is part of the collection of the Library of Congress.

I, too, have retired from my regular day gig. Besides photographing again, I am getting an enormous boot out of exhibiting the superb work of Bill Gottlieb and that of many other veterans and the new and up-and-coming photographers. For years, many of us couldn't give away our prints. Now we are getting a full measure of aesthetic appreciation, and, as we see, it is even possible to have one's work acquired by the Library of Congress. What a marvelous turn of events! Congratulations to you, Bill!

—*Lee Tanner*

THE GOLDEN AGE of JAZZ

Chapter 1

THAT OLD-TIME JAZZ

During the '30s and '40s there were still plenty of working musicians who had been around when jazz was beginning. They were authentic pioneers but not as old as sometimes depicted. Since most of them were born in the 1890s, the average "old-timer" was still under fifty.

These veterans were a colorful breed, often with extravagant personalities that added pizzazz to their jazz. Musically, however, they were conservative, usually clinging to traditional styles as if the styles were security blankets—which in a way they were, for this was the music the fans expected of them. Old-timers departed from it at their peril.

Although old-time jazz had limited appeal during the Golden Age, it did enjoy a substantial renaissance, thanks partly to the general enthusiasm for hot music generated among audiences by the popular swing bands of the era.

The playing of traditional jazz was not entirely confined to the old-timers. The music attracted a number of disciples, some of them only in their teens and all of them fanatical. They were the play-it-like-it-was musicians who, along with equally fervid listeners, found in the old-time jazz just the chord that suited them.

Louis Armstrong.

Willie "The Lion" Smith

OLD-TIMER WILLIE "THE LION" SMITH never became one of the paramount kings of jazz, but he couldn't have handled himself in a more regal manner; he dressed splendidly, walked with majestic dignity, held court grandly with his fans, and—with royal self-esteem—habitually referred to himself in the third person. "The Lion is here," he would announce on entering a room. While playing, The Lion sat on the piano stool as if it were a throne. And if the music was going well, he'd swivel sideways on the stool, the better to address his loyal subjects, and issue a series of lordly observations like: "The Lion is laying it down real good tonight!"

The Lion's full name was William Henry Joseph Bonaparte Bertholoff Smith. With all that to choose from, how did he end up calling himself The Lion? The first time I asked, he said he was given his nickname by another legendary pianist, James P. Johnson, in recognition of The Lion's domineering attitude. (In return, The Lion called James P. "The Brute," not because of Johnson's personality, which was pleasant, but because of his imposing body topped by an oversized head.)

About a year after giving me that account of his name, The Lion came up with an entirely different version: "In the First World War, I was a gunner in a Negro brigade. When our colonel wanted some of us to man a French seventy-five, I volunteered and was up front firing for forty-five days, without relief. The colonel promoted me to sergeant and told everyone I was a 'lion' with a gun. The name stuck."

The Lion once gave a similar account to Timmie Rosenkrantz, a Danish baron turned jazznik. The Lion ended his story with this beautiful coda: "It was a tough war, Timmie, and I'm proud and happy I won it."

Still another time, The Lion gave me a third version of how he got his name. "I'm Jewish. I was bar mitzvahed, speak Yiddish fluently . . . the whole megillah. I tried to become a rabbi, but because of prejudice the best I could do was study to be a cantor. A cantor's job is mostly music. Naturally, I was great—so great that the rest of the class called me the Lion of Judea."

The Lion then showed me his calling card. On one side was his name, Willie "The Lion" Smith, with his address, phone number, and the title "The Hebrew Cantor," all printed in English. On the other side of the card was the equivalent information in Hebrew.

The Lion's outrageous flamboyance never obscured his talent as a musician. On jump tunes, his rock-solid stride piano could be the driving force behind a band. Yet he could immediately follow with a delicate solo, perhaps his own charming composition "Echoes of Spring."

The Lion was particularly known for his strong left hand. Appropriately, he had a ready roar for piano players who couldn't make full use of all ten fingers. "What's the matter, man—your left hand crippled? Here, let me show you how to do it."

And he did show plenty of piano players "how to do it." Dozens of first-rate jazz pianists acknowledge their debt to him. One of his "students," Duke Ellington, paid tribute by composing and recording "Portrait of The Lion."

Yet it's The Lion's grandiose personality, more than his superb musicianship, that I now most often recall. There's the time the two of us, in Washington, drove by taxi to the Howard Theater, where he was performing. When we arrived and got out of the cab, the driver asked for the fare. Before responding, The Lion slowly and deliberately shepherded me through the stage door, then turned and imperiously announced, "The Lion never pays for taxis!"

The driver was too flabbergasted to react. Unchallenged, The Lion joined me inside, after closing the stage door firmly.

(RIGHT) *James P. Johnson, with Freddie Moore at drums and Fess Williams with clarinet.*

(OPPOSITE) *Leadbelly.*

James P. Johnson

JAMES P. JOHNSON DIDN'T HAVE the hubris of his crony The Lion, but he was nonetheless an imposing and important person, probably the most influential jazz piano player performing between the reigns of Scott Joplin and Earl Hines. His disciples, including Fats Waller, dominated a generation of keyboard artists. Jimmy was also a composer. He wrote jazz pieces, a symphony, and one of the top pop hits of the '20s, "Charleston."

By the time I got to know James P., he had suffered a paralyzing stroke. Although largely recovered, he had become relatively subdued, according to friends who recalled his vibrant days. But, subdued or not, he continued to be regarded as one of jazz's venerable masters.

When I left the music business to enter the audiovisual field, it was James P. Johnson who, with a combo that included Freddy Moore, Fess Williams, and Joe Thomas, played at my office opening—which is where I took the picture shown above.

Huddie "Leadbelly" Ledbetter

LEADBELLY, A FABULOUS BLUES SINGER and guitarist, killed one man, maybe two. During his last incarceration, this time in a Louisiana prison, he was the star at an entertainment given for the visiting state governor. Leadbelly used his rough but beguiling voice, his twelve-string guitar, and some improvised lyrics to deliver not only music but a message: "Hey, Gov, get me outta here." He didn't get a hoped-for pardon but did win a shortened term, also gaining thereby enough publicity to eventually launch a memorable concert career.

In 1940, for the first time, I attended one of his performances. I knew his background and expected to see someone who looked fierce and formidable. Instead, he appeared

Bunk Johnson and Leadbelly; clarinetist George Lewis, bottom left; bassist Alcide "Slow Drag" Pavageau, rear.

mild, almost gentle. Normally, I would have tried to capture this quality with my camera; but, devilishly, I chose to accommodate my preconception: I manipulated my flashbulb to produce the sinister chiaroscuro portrait you see on the previous page.

The "real" Leadbelly can be seen above in a rare pairing with an equally legendary musician, Bunk Johnson.

William "Bunk" Johnson

BUNK JOHNSON WAS AN ESTABLISHED
New Orleans trumpet player at about the
turn of the century. But in the 1930s, in the
depths of the Great Depression, music jobs
became scarce. His miseries multiplied when
he had to sell his horn and, even worse for a
trumpet player, lost his teeth. Discouraged,
he quit music and became a field hand in
New Iberia, Louisiana.

Years later he was rediscovered by a jazz
historian, Bill Russell, who bought him false
teeth and replaced his trumpet. By the middle
1940s, Bunk was back in music and thriving.
Audiences came to see and hear him as if he
were a supposedly extinct creature miraculously
found alive—a veritable human coelacanth.

I caught Bunk in New York when he and
a band of other old-timers were working a
Second Avenue bar mitzvah hall that, on
non–holy days, was used for secular events.
While listening to the Johnson band, I no-
ticed a very young woman hanging around
the bandstand and asked Bunk who she was.
"I got me a wife," he answered, as if he had
just returned from a shopping trip. He asked
me to photograph the two of them. I used
an old-fashioned pose: husband seated, wife
standing behind him (in this instance, looking uncomfortable). My caption? Simply
"Bunk Johnson and bride."

William "Bunk" Johnson and bride.

(RIGHT) Warren "Baby" Dodds was percussionist at one time or another for many of the top traditional leaders, including King Oliver, Louis Armstrong, Jelly Roll Morton, and Bunk Johnson. His elder brother, Johnny, an influential clarinetist, died in 1940.

(MIDDLE RIGHT) Albert Nicholas played a classic, supple New Orleans clarinet. He appeared with countless traditional and swing bands; and, like his fellow reedman Sidney Bechet, he was appreciated even more in Europe than in America.

(LOWER RIGHT) George "Pops" Foster was probably the musician most responsible for the tuba's being replaced by the string bass, a far more flexible instrument.

(OPPOSITE) Sidney Bechet, the eminent soprano saxophonist, was an important jazzman in America, an even more important one in Europe. In 1919, Ernest Ansermet, the Swiss symphony orchestra conductor, pronounced him a musical giant. In France, Bechet was a national hero; after his death a statue of him was erected on the Riviera.

MORE OLD-TIMERS CAME FROM New Orleans than from any other city. The four shown here were working musicians as far back as 1910 and were still busy through the 1940s.

Old-time jazz (New Orleans style and its variants) was created by blacks, and into the 1940s, older black musicians continued to play it. But not the young ones. Young blacks, as well as progressive young whites, would not, as a rule, even listen to traditional jazz. They favored more modern forms.

The musicians and audiences who did support the old sounds were mostly whites—typically elderly, middle-class whites. They were the ones, for example, who vigorously supported Dixieland music, a style closely related to the New Orleans brand.

Incidentally, this split in the jazz world continues to exist: on one side, favoring traditional styles, are older whites and older blacks; on the other side, favoring modern styles, are almost all younger blacks and a majority of young whites. There are other splinter groups too, such as the one I belong to: I like just about all styles.

On the East Coast during the Golden Age, one of the most noted of the young, white, old-time-jazz practitioners was Bob Wilber and his Wildcats, an enthusiastic group first composed largely of high school students

Bob Wilber and his mentor, Sidney Bechet. Sidney, as usual, is playing a soprano sax; but this time, Bob is on clarinet.

from Scarsdale, a fashionable suburb of New York City. (On the West Coast, there were the Lu Watters and Turk Murphy bands.) Wilber, a clarinetist and soprano saxophonist, was a disciple of the great venerable Sidney Bechet and became a prominent traditional-style jazzman, as did others among the Wildcats. (One, trumpeter Johnny Glasel, became president of Local 802 in New York, whose membership entailed the largest segment of the American Federation of Musicians.)

During much of the Golden Age, the centers of traditional-style jazz in New York, and perhaps in the world, were three nightclubs: Jimmy Ryan's on 52nd Street, Nick's in Greenwich Village, and—just a few blocks away—Eddie Condon's.

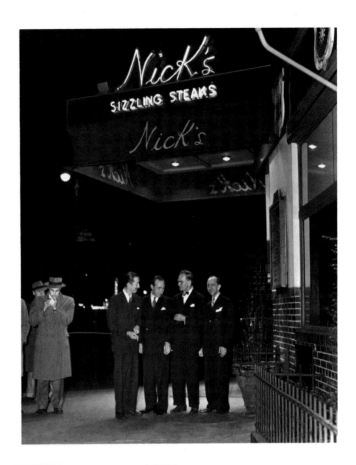

Nick's, with four sizzling favorites: Pee Wee Russell, Muggsy Spanier, Miff Mole, and Joe Grauso.

A session at Jimmy Ryan's featuring Wilbur De Paris, trombone; his brother Sidney, trumpet; Eddie Barefield, clarinet; Charlie Traeger, bass; and Sammy Price, piano.

Francis "Muggsy" Spanier was one of the most sought-after cornetists of the period. With both open horn and plunger mute, he was marvelously full-bodied and precise.

THE BANDS THAT PLAYED THOSE SPOTS were small combos with shifting personnel. Although individuals sometimes became identified with one or another of the clubs, most of them in the course of a couple of years played at least one gig at Ryan's and Nick's and Condon's.

The music at all of them was characteristically Dixieland; but on occasion, more modern sounds could be heard. Many of the sidemen took periodic leave of the Dixieland circuit to work with big swing bands. And I often found Jack Lesberg, one of the Condon "regulars," playing bass with symphony orchestras.

Two of the most prominent members of the Condon crew were Mugsy Spanier and Pee Wee Russell.

"Pee Wee" Russell had a mournful face, a mumbling voice, and a growling clarinet. But on him it looked good. Pee Wee was one of the best and most loved musicians in jazz.

Eddie Condon.

Eddie Condon's club was newer and shorter-lived than Ryan's or Nick's, but it was the liveliest of the three, thanks largely to its proprietor and permanent floating guitarist, Eddie Condon himself.

Eddie was reputed to be an outstanding musician; he appeared on some historic records and won two *Down Beat* polls. But by the time I got to know him, his best efforts went into promoting music at concerts and at his club, and into playing the role of "a widely quoted personality." (Practically everyone talked about his comment on Hugues Panassie, the French jazz critic who came to the United States and appraised our music. Said Condon: "Who is he to tell us about

jazz? We don't tell Frenchmen how to jump on a grape.")

As far as I know, Eddie never took a guitar solo. He stuck to ensemble playing, when he played at all. Often as not, the guitar chair at Condon's was empty. Ever the diligent proprietor, Eddie was frequently off talking with patrons or running quality control tests at his bar. But his absence didn't matter. The musicians of the day, playing mostly New Orleans and Dixieland standards, could do just fine by themselves.

The Condon crew consisted of twenty or so illustrious jazzmen. Some of them are seen on the following pages.

Eddie Condon's, with a typical line-up: (from left) Pee Wee Russell, Max Kaminsky, Wild Bill Davison, Jack Lesberg (rear), George Brunis, Bud Freeman, and Freddie Ohms. Note Eddie Condon's empty chair, in front of Pee Wee.

(RIGHT) Lawrence "Bud" Freeman could fit in anywhere. He was at times a sideman with some of the sweetest pop bands, and at others a featured hot soloist with the Benny Goodman and Tommy Dorsey orchestras. The greatest mark of his versatility was being accepted by the Dixielanders; he was the first tenor saxophonist admitted to their ranks.

(BELOW) Joe Sullivan was the best known of the Dixieland pianists, but he also was active as an accompanist for singers such as Bing Crosby.

(LEFT) Jack Lesberg, Max Kaminsky, and Michael "Peanuts" Hucko were normally among the more serious of the Condonites. Max played trumpet; Peanuts, clarinet.

(BELOW) George Wettling, though one of the busiest drummers of the era, made time for serious painting. A student of the abstract expressionist Stuart Davis, George hoped his painting would prove as successful as his drumming, but his hopes were in vain.

Here are three traditionalists:

(RIGHT) George Brunis and Tony Parenti were regulars in the trombone and clarinet chairs at Condon's.

(BELOW) Joseph "Wingy" Manone, a popular trumpeter and leader, put more effort into playing clown than into playing music, but he could be a fine instrumentalist. Along with Louis Prima, Wingy was the best known of the white imitators of Louis Armstrong.

In his role as clown, Wingy played up his homely looks. I went along with him in this close-up, which initially accompanied a newspaper story that began: "A gargoyle broke off from the back wall of Town Hall and walked towards me. It was Wingy Manone."

(ABOVE) Milton "Mezz" Mezzrow had more significance as a crusader for traditional jazz than as a musician. He was also an active promoter of black culture and called himself a "voluntary Negro." His book, Really the Blues, was one of the first of many autobiographies by jazzmen.

(LEFT) Art Hodes was for a time just another good piano player. He also became well known by crusading for old-time jazz. Hodes pushed his cause by organizing various traditional-style combos and by touting New Orleans and Dixieland music while working as a radio disc jockey and as a magazine writer.

Chapter 2

SATCHMO AND THE DUKE: BEYOND CATEGORY

During the Golden Age, the pantheon of jazz greats was crowded with musical giants: Basie, Cole, Davis, Fitzgerald, Gillespie, Goodman, Hawkins, Hines, Holiday, Lunceford, Parker, Shaw, Tatum, Teagarden, Young, and more. Still, there were two others enthroned even above them: Daniel Louis Armstrong and Edward Kennedy Ellington—Satchmo and the Duke.

Satchmo and the Duke: one the greatest jazz instrumentalist who had thus far appeared, the other the foremost creator of orchestral jazz. One raised in a New Orleans slum and in a home for delinquents, the other raised in a solid, middle-class Washington, D.C., environment and so pampered that "I must have been six years old before my feet touched the ground."

Famous as far back as the early '20s, Satchmo and the Duke cannot be regarded as exclusively the products of the Golden Age. However, throughout much of the '30s and '40s, they loomed above the entire jazz scene. They were beyond time—and beyond category.

Louis Armstrong.

(RIGHT) Louis in a "thin" phase.

Louis "Satchmo" Armstrong

IT'S DIFFICULT TO THINK JAZZ without thinking Armstrong. Almost from that moment in 1922 when young Louis left New Orleans to join King Oliver in Chicago, his electrifying technique and direct emotional intensity overwhelmed the jazz world. Thousands of cornet and trumpet players adopted his way of playing as best they could. Equal numbers of trombonists, saxophonists, and piano players adapted their attack to resemble his.

Then there's Satchmo's singing. His voice was hoarse, gutteral, totally unmusical by conventional standards; but by transferring his phrasing and feelings from horn to voice, he became the best of jazz vocalists. Many imitators followed, even when it meant masking a legitimate voice box to affect one lined with gravel.

During much of the Golden Age, Louis Armstrong shifted from serious musician to amusing entertainer. He clowned, showed off spectacular high notes, sang sticky pop songs, became a movie star. But he never could completely conceal his musical talent. Satchmo's most banal performances were peppered with flecks of his genius.

Despite his lofty perch, Satch was easily approached and as genial offstage as on. Almost everyone with whom he had much contact regarded this open, earthy man as a friend, even though he often couldn't remember names and called most everyone Pops. (In turn, almost everyone called him Pops, though he also answered to Louis, Satch, and Satchmo—the last two being diminutives of Satchelmouth.)

Satch, like so many ordinary humans, had a weight problem and had both fat periods and lean. As a prodigious consumer of red beans and rice (he often ended his many amusing letters with "Red beans and ricely yours"), Louis was more often fat than lean.

Louis had a personal diet that he touted. It was heavy on Pluto Water, a dynamite laxative that was popular years ago. Genial Satch kept in his inside jacket pocket copies of the diet, which he liked to hand out to friends who he thought needed it.

Louis and I happened to have the same dentist. A few months before Louis died, I found him entering the dentist's office as I was about to leave. The great man's famous chops were hurting and, from the way he looked, so were many other parts of him.

Bad as Satch must have felt, he was his usual gracious self. We chatted about old

Armstrong backstage. Particularly note the pile of handkerchiefs; when performing, he almost always had one in hand, to wipe his brow. Also note the bottle of Pluto Water.

times until it was time for me to depart. Just before I was about to disappear through the door, he called out, "Hey, Pops, wait!" I turned toward him and could see that he had been sizing up my hulk. He then pulled a sheet of paper from his inside jacket pocket and handed it to me. "There's this diet, man. The greatest. Try it."

And I might have. But I just couldn't find a store that still sold Pluto Water.

By 1929 Louis Armstrong, already world famous, had given up playing the small-combo jazz that had been so musically rewarding. Instead he became, in effect, a solo entertainer. There continued to be Armstrong orchestras, but they were really the bands of others that Louis merely fronted. The sidemen kept in the background while Louis did his thing, projecting his fabulous personality more than his fabulous music.

Then in the mid '40s, Satch formed a small group of all-stars; he returned to the format that had first brought him fame. Once again the jazz poured out, although Satch still managed to get in some clowning, make some movies, and come up with smash-hit pop records like "Mack the Knife" and "Hello, Dolly."

The photographs on this and the next few pages show some of the later-day stars who were associated with Armstrong.

(RIGHT) Henry "Red" Allen, a trumpeter with a slashing, raucous attack, led his own small group through much of the '40s but frequently backed Satchmo, especially on concert dates.

(BELOW) Jack "Jay C." Higginbotham was a trombonist with a powerful drive. He was a perfect match for Red Allen, with whom he was frequently teamed. For several years Jay C. was one of Armstrong's regulars, often alongside Red.

At this concert in New York's
Town Hall, Louis's group consisted
of Jack Teagarden, trombone;
Dick Cary, piano; Bobby Hackett,
trumpet; Peanuts Hucko, clarinet;
Bob Haggart, bass; and Sid
Catlett, drums.

(OPPOSITE) Earl "Fatha" Hines played piano with Louis Armstrong for several years in the late 1940s. More significantly, Fatha worked with Satch back in 1927, when, reacting to Louis's blazing talent, he revolutionized jazz piano playing by using his right hand to play trumpet-style, single-note lines in the Armstrong manner. For the next two decades, almost every young piano player—most notably Teddy Wilson—fell into Fatha's groove.

During part of the Golden Age, Fatha was a bandleader and the composer of such music as "Rosetta," his biggest hit. He also established a reputation for encouraging young musicians; at one time his band included Dizzy Gillespie, Charlie Parker, Sarah Vaughan, and Billy Eckstine.

(LEFT) Sidney "Big Sid" Catlett, long an Armstrong stalwart, was a gifted and versatile drummer. He was one of the few "older" swing percussionists who easily made the transition to bop.

(BELOW) Arthur "Zutty" Singleton was a member of Armstrong's early, legendary Hot Five recording group, as well as more recent Armstrong combos.

Weldon J. "Jack" Teagarden was the preeminent trombonist of the Golden Age. After giving up his own band, he began a long association with Armstrong. Like Satch, Jack sang jazz almost as well as he played it. On vocal duets his soft, lazy Texan drawl proved an ideal complement to Satch's robust growling.

Edward Kennedy "Duke" Ellington

I WAS ALWAYS AWED BY DUKE ELLINGTON. Everything about him dazzled me—his music, of course, and also his energy, his hipness, his appearance. Consider his appearance: handsome, elegant, suave, sophisticated. Those are the kinds of adjectives used to describe the way he looked. He was a natural. But he had help, too, as was apparent when I met him one day in the Paramount Theater dressing room.

Duke had just come out of the shower. I couldn't help noticing that when he was completely unadorned, he obviously had an overly ample waist. Suave? Elegant? Not quite. But once he applied some baby powder and various other emollients, selected one of his twenty-five suits, added an expensive shirt and tie, and assumed his confident bearing . . . Presto! He suddenly *was* suave, elegant, and all the rest. Magic!

Ellington's magic filled his music, too. As a writer of popular tunes, he turned out such hits as "Mood Indigo," "Solitude," "Sophisticated Lady," "In a Sentimental Mood," and "I Got It Bad and That Ain't Good." As a pianist, Duke was something less than spectacular, but his playing was just right for the orchestral role he assigned to the keyboard. Which brings us to the orchestra itself. Duke's instrument was acknowledged to *be* his orchestra. He "played the band." And what a player! He created jazz that had more colors, more textures, more surprises than were found anywhere else in jazz.

The Ellington orchestra didn't have the unadulterated drive of, say, the Basie or Lunceford aggregations. But it nonetheless had a powerful beat. One of Duke's hits was "It Don't Mean a Thing If It Ain't Got That Swing." Duke rarely ignored the advice.

Around 1940, Ellington's output was particularly memorable. It included an amazing cluster of recorded instrumentals: "Jack the Bear," "Harlem Air Shaft," "Concerto for Cootie," "Ko Ko," "Caravan," "Conga Brava," "Warm Valley," "Cotton Tail," and "Never No Lament." (Later, two of those instrumentals were given lyrics and became hits under the titles "Do Nothing Till You Hear from Me" and "Don't Get Around Much Anymore.")

(ABOVE) *Duke and, to his left, the author, in the author's Washington home, 1941. With them are (left) Ahmet Ertegun and (right) his brother Nesuhi. The Erteguns were jazz fans and the sons of the Turkish ambassador to the United States. They later were pashas in the music industry: Ahmet became the major founder of Atlantic Records (others were Herb Abramson and a Turkish-American dentist, Vahdi Sabit); Nesuhi became head of WEA (Warner-Electra-Atlantic International).*

(LEFT) *Duke was a piano player. But in a meaningful sense, his instrument was his orchestra.*

During the Golden Age, playing with the Duke Ellington orchestra was the ultimate goal of just about every black musician. Being tapped by His Highness the Duke meant being recognized as one of the world's outstanding instrumentalists. It was like getting a Pulitzer Prize.

Among other dividends for Ellington sidemen was the special attention they received; the band's arrangements were written with specific players in mind. Although each of Duke's musicians had to subordinate himself to some extent to the Ellington style, he was still given an extraordinary opportunity to show off his talents, thanks to those tailor-made charts.

With benefits like these, musicians did their best not only to get into the orchestra but also to stay in. Leaving the Duke voluntarily, at least during the Golden Age, was almost unthinkable, and personnel changes were rare. When, late in 1940, Cootie

Williams quit to go with Benny Goodman for more money, it was such a shocker that the Raymond Scott orchestra immortalized it with a recording, "When Cootie Left the Duke."

Whitney Balliett, who covers jazz for the *New Yorker,* describes the relations between the Duke and his men: "Hodges or Bigard or Ben Webster would give him eight or twelve beautiful bars and those would pass through his extraordinary head and come out as 'Mood Indigo' or 'Sophisticated Lady'. . . . The Ellington afflatus was dangerous. It drained his musicians, and at the same time, because so many of his tunes were written specifically for them, it spoiled them. When longtime sidemen left, they either dropped into obscurity or, thirsting for the Master's attention, returned to the fold."

Shown on these pages are many of the more prominent Ellingtonians who were in the fold during the Golden Age.

Guitarist Django Reinhardt backstage with part of the Ellington orchestra during a joint concert tour. From left: Al Sears, Shelton Hemphill, Junior Raglin, Reinhardt, Lawrence Brown, Harry Carney, and Johnny Hodges.

(LEFT) William "Cat" Anderson was the band's high-note specialist. When he was about to screech one, he liked to point out where the note would go.

(BELOW) John "Rabbit" Hodges had a completely deadpan expression, yet out of his horn came the most sensuous, most voluptuous sounds in jazz. Almost all of Johnny's career was spent in Duke's reed section, although he formed his own band for a while, taking along another Ellingtonian, tenor man Al Sears (shown in the background), as musical director.

(ABOVE) William "Sonny" Greer joined forces with Duke in 1919, in Washington: two sharp young cats out to show the world their stuff.

(RIGHT) Ray Nance, ever the entertainer, jived around doing his thing as singer, dancer, and trumpeter. But when he came to grips with his violin, he became serious. Suddenly the jive was gone.

Harry Carney joined Ellington when he was only sixteen years old and remained with the band until his death more than forty-seven years later. He was for a long time the only great baritone saxophonist in jazz. Russell Procope is on the left.

(RIGHT) Ben Webster was the first tenor sax player to be featured by Duke. His driving Kansas City horn added a new sound to the band. Starting with "Cotton Tail," Ellington regularly wrote music that displayed Ben's exciting tenor.

(BELOW) Rex Stewart, an amusing and intelligent fellow, frequently expressed himself with witty cornet playing. In "Boy Meets Horn," Rex created a novel and much-imitated "squeezed" tone by depressing his cornet valves only halfway.

(OPPOSITE) William "Swee' Pea" Strayhorn was only twenty-three when he was brought into the band to back up Ellington as arranger and pianist. He successfully met this formidable challenge and went on to become Duke's alter ego. Strayhorn's creative output became almost indistinguishable from the boss's. "Take the 'A' Train," a Swee' Pea composition that sounded "all Ellington," emerged as the band's theme song.

(OPPOSITE) Charles "Cootie" Williams was the Ellington super-star whose growling trumpet provided much of the "jungle" sound that the band often featured. I once asked Cootie how he came by his famous growl. I was hoping he'd reveal some profound motivations, something about deep-rooted social torments pouring out of his horn. "Well," Cootie answered, "I was hired by Duke to take Bubber Miley's place, and Duke told me, 'Growl like Bubber.' So I growled."

(TOP LEFT) Barney Bigard, who had played with King Oliver, added his fluid New Orleans clarinet to the Ellington palette. Barney's swooping lines became one of the band's most distinctive sounds.

(MIDDLE LEFT) Jimmy Hamilton had the formidable assignment of taking the place of Barney Bigard. He managed to pull it off beautifully.

(LOWER LEFT) Oscar Pettiford was one of a list of distinguished Ellington bassists. He also became one of the early champions of bop.

THERE HAS NEVER BEEN A JAZZ ORCHESTRA with so many brilliant sidemen, each a star by himself, yet each an integral element in the whole organization—like Juan Tizol, the Puerto Rican valve trombonist who added a Latin flavor and wrote the exotic "Caravan," or Lawrence Brown, part of the section called "God's trombones," or a succession of great bassists (sometimes two at a time), including Jimmy Blanton and Oscar Pettiford.

(RIGHT) Lawrence Brown.

(BELOW) Juan Tizol.

(LEFT) Evans "Tyree" Glenn, an Ellingtonian for five years, had an odd double specialty: trombone and vibes. Versatile Tyree was also an actor, on the side.

(BELOW) An early 1940s Ellington orchestra.

Chapter 3

SWING AND THE BIRTH OF THE GOLDEN AGE

The Golden Age of Jazz, like most eras, came in slowly, almost imperceptibly. Then suddenly the world took notice. It was here!

Some say its ultimate arrival can be pinpointed to that day in the summer of 1935 when the Benny Goodman orchestra, after a dismal series of unsuccessful cross-country one-nighters, arrived at the Palomar Ballroom in Los Angeles. To its surprise, the band was greeted hysterically by an overflow crowd of young people!

The Los Angeles audience had been prepared for the Goodman style. They had been listening to Benny's band on a network show called Let's Dance, *and the music had grabbed them but good. When they finally heard the music first-hand, boom! An explosion.*

Why, until then, had the band's tour flopped? Because of time zone differences, the Let's Dance *program reached the East and the Midwest at too late an hour to be heard by the young people of those regions—hence their failure to respond as the westerners did to the band's personal appearance. However, within a year of the Palomar date, jazz, under the name of "swing," had overwhelmed every part of the country, even the world.*

Jazz had, of course, been with us long before Goodman's triumph, but it was largely confined to special groups: blacks, a few white musicians, some white fans, and a handful of critics, nearly all of them European. (Jazz had a special fascination for European intellectuals.)

As for the so-called Jazz Age of the '20s, that title was a musical misnomer. The "jazz" that most Americans heard at that time was usually not the real thing. Paul Whiteman, then the "King of Jazz," played virtually none of it. Al Jolson, the popular "Jazz Singer," sang literally none of it.

But underground at least, the number of true believers was growing. By the time Benny Goodman came on the scene, a considerable amount of authentic hot music was being played. There were notable black orchestras like those of Duke Ellington, Louis Armstrong, Jimmie Lunceford, Fletcher Henderson, and Bennie Moten. There were or had recently been fairly good white bands, too, like those of Ben Pollack, Red Nichols, Ray Noble, and Glen Gray.

Bit by bit, real jazz began creeping into the consciousness of typical young Americans. By 1935 they were just about ready. Then Benny hit Palomar and, at last, it arrived!

Benny Goodman.

(BELOW) Goodman was the first important jazz musician to play straight classical music in public. It was an interesting venture but not very successful artistically or financially. Here he's rehearsing for a concert conducted by Leonard Bernstein.

Benny Goodman

BENNY GOODMAN WAS THE RIGHT MAN at the right time. A superlative musician with glittering improvisational techniques, he was also a relentlessly ambitious careerist who probed in many directions, searching for avenues to success. Through fortuitous timing, he found the right one.

His great good fortune was using jazz as his vehicle. It was a bandwagon that millions were just ready to board. "He was," wrote critic Leonard Feather in his *Encyclopedia of Jazz,* "the first to adopt an uncompromising jazz style, one that took both standard and popular material and turned it into the idiom that became known as swing, thus starting an entire new era."

Here are some of his other successes:

He made the clarinet, at least for a while, one of the most popular of instruments.

He hired dozens of superb but unknown musicians, gaining for them the attention they deserved.

He popularized chamber jazz by featuring instrumental trios and other small units.

And he employed a number of blacks, using his prestige to break down racial taboos so that the mixing of black and white musicians became possible and even commonplace.

A dazzling list of accomplishments!

Benny Goodman was surely a tower in the world of jazz, but he was also a terror among those with whom he worked. He was constantly accused of being cold, insensitive, thoughtless. He tended to ignore his sidemen for long periods; then the moment he disapproved of their playing, he'd shoot them down with the awesome stare known as The Ray.

Understandably, there was a high turnover rate in the Goodman orchestra. For a long time the gag line on 52nd Street was that at any one

time there were three Goodman orchestras: the one he had just fired, the one he had just hired, and the one that was still with him.

Many of Benny's detractors maintained that much of Benny's glory rightfully belonged to John Hammond, a socially conscious jazz devotee who frequently gave advice to Benny (and whose sister married Benny). John was undoubtedly responsible for many of Benny's "discoveries," as well as for getting Benny to hire blacks. (Hammond, often working in unofficial capacities, also played crucial roles in building the careers of a dozen other top stars, from Count Basie and Billie Holiday to Bob Dylan and Bruce Springsteen.)

It was Hammond who, in 1935, persuaded Gene Krupa to join Benny's band. In his autobiography, *John Hammond on Record,* John tells how he had to twist Gene's arm—hard—to get him to come, for Krupa had

already had experience with Goodman and didn't want more of the same. Gene relented and joined Benny, but he could never do more than tolerate his boss. Still, Gene, like other ex-Goodman sidemen, had to admit that, personal issues aside, Benny was a great benefactor of music.

Nat Shapiro and Nat Hentoff, in their book *Hear Me Talkin to Ya,* have this quotation from Krupa: "Benny built himself a band playing musicians' music. . . . It allowed us to play the way we honestly wanted to play, with good pay and before huge, appreciative audiences. In the days before the Goodman era, we played that way, too, but in smaller bands and with no similar success. . . . For all that Benny did for music, for jazz, for musicians, and for me, I, for one, doff my cap in a salute of sincere appreciation."

In my own encounters with Benny, he followed form. Although he never shot me with

(ABOVE LEFT) Benny on the bandstand with saxophonist Vido Musso and drummer Sid Catlett.

(ABOVE RIGHT & ABOVE) Harry James.

(RIGHT & LOWER RIGHT) Lionel Hampton. Hamp's supercharged energies and blazing talents catapulted him to stardom. His specialty was vibes, but he also played flashy drums and piano. On piano, he used only his index fingers, flailing them like vibraphone mallets. (A second pianist usually filled in the "left hand" parts.)

(BELOW LEFT) Gene Krupa was the most popular of the jazz drummers. His solo on "Sing, Sing, Sing," while he was with the Benny Goodman orchestra, was a sensation and helped make him the first percussionist to become a jazz giant.

The Ray, he never exactly exuded charm, either. In each interview he answered questions with as few syllables as possible: a couple of "no's," a "yes" or two, several grunts, and here and there some short sentences. For lack of verbal tinder, the interviews quickly burned out.

But, as Gene Krupa said, for all he's done for jazz, I doff my hat in sincere appreciation.

Dozens of outstanding musicians passed in and out of the Benny Goodman orchestra. The BG alumni association became one of the most distinguished societies in the music world, with many of its members moving up to lead orchestras of their own.

The most successful of the ex-Goodman sidemen were Gene Krupa, Harry James, and Lionel Hampton. For much of the Golden Age each was the most popular musician on his respective instrument, and the orchestras they led sometimes challenged that of Benny himself.

(LEFT) Jess Stacy was another of Benny's fine pianists. He played with the full band, while Teddy Wilson was featured with the Trio and Quartet.

(BELOW LEFT) Melvin "Mel" Powell, a notable piano player who joined Benny in 1941, is shown with his wife, actress Martha Scott.

(BELOW RIGHT) Teddy Wilson, an impeccable pianist, was the first black musician hired by Goodman and an outstanding keyboard man playing in the Earl Hines tradition. Teddy is at left, drummer Zutty Singleton at right.

William "Count" Basie

FOR THOSE WHO LIKED THEIR SWING DIRECT
and to the point, the greatest of the bands
belonged to Count Basie. John S. Wilson,
jazz critic of the *New York Times,* put it this
way: "At the height of the Swing Era, this
was the swing band incarnate."

Count Basie and his musicians generated
a powerful drive that used crescendos of riffs
interspersed with blazing solos, all of it further propelled by the best rhythm section in
the business. It was a comparatively uncom-

plicated style, but it was irresistibly com-
pelling . . . and glorious.

In the midst of all this throbbing, unfet-
tered power, the Count's own playing seemed
anomalous—delicate, sparse, completely un-
derstated. Yet it was perfectly suited for its job.
His keyboard notes may have been economi-
cal in number, but each was exquisitely timed
to give a subtle but unmistakable rhythmic
kick that spurred the other musicians.

One week, late in 1938, both the Count
Basie and the Bob Crosby orchestras were in
Washington. I was able to obtain the use of

(OPPOSITE TOP) Count Basie, Ray Bauduc, Bob Haggart, and Herschel Evans on the stage of the Howard. Bauduc and Haggart had only recently recorded their famous drum-bass duet, "Big Noise from Winnetka." Evans, a highly regarded tenor man, was to die only a few months later, at age thirty, becoming an instant legend.

(OPPOSITE BOTTOM) An incongruous but sensational reed section: Herschel Evans, Eddie Miller, Lester Young, and Matty Matlock.

(LEFT) Lester "Pres" Young was the most distinguished and influential of Basie's many fine sidemen.

(BELOW) When playing, Lester was easily recognizable, even from the rear, because of the novel way he held his tenor horn. He was equally recognizable for his laid-back sound—a departure from the style of Coleman Hawkins, whose attacking style had been dominant.

the Howard Theater stage "after hours" and persuaded both groups to come together for a jam session. There was just one problem—the Crosby band played Dixieland, a style as far from that of the Basie band as it was possible to get and still be jazz. Could they fit together musically? They could. Their differences were insignificant compared with their fundamental similarities. That evening, fantastic music was made.

During its long history, the Count Basie orchestra went through several distinct periods. Each could claim a number of musical stars. Here are pictures of some of them.

(ABOVE) Oran "Lips" Page, shown here sitting in with Sidney Bechet, played with the Basie band in its Kansas City days. He then went on to spark other groups, including his own. (Back row: left, Freddie Moore; right, Lloyd Phillips.)

(RIGHT) Wilbur "Buck" Clayton, trumpeter and arranger, was featured on most of Basie's best-known recordings. When this photo was taken, he had left the Count to lead his own group. Ted Kelly is on trombone; Ken Kersey on piano; Benny Fonville on bass; Scoville Brown on clarinet; and Shep Shepherd on drums. Kersey was an early bop man.

(LEFT) William "Dickie" Wells and Henry "Benny" Morton (BELOW), both veteran jazzmen, were the trombone soloists during Basie's early "glory" years.

(BELOW) The pulsating power of the Lunceford orchestra was particularly apparent in "battles of swing." In one contest, at which I officiated, the Krupa band, which by itself seemed so solid, sounded thin and tinny when juxtaposed with the Lunceford band. Shown here are Lunceford, the author, and Krupa.

(OPPOSITE) Jimmie Lunceford "all alone," soon after several key sidemen had left him.

James Melvin "Jimmie" Lunceford

FOR SEVERAL YEARS, BEGINNING IN 1934, Jimmie Lunceford had the band with the biggest beat in the business. Much of the credit belonged to the distinctive arrangements of trumpeter Sy Oliver and pianist Ed Wilcox, together with the musicianship of many outstanding sidemen. In the mid '40s, most of the key musicians left and the band declined. Jimmie himself died in 1947.

(ABOVE) Sy Oliver, whose arrangements set the style for the Lunceford band, later did the same for Tommy Dorsey.

(RIGHT) James "Trummy" Young. His out-of-breath singing style and robust trombone were strong points in the Lunceford band.

(LEFT) Willie Smith, alto sax, was the outstanding instrumentalist in the Lunceford organization. He's shown here on a post-Lunceford recording date. The trombonist is Juan Tizol, who had recently left Duke Ellington.

(BELOW) Joe Thomas and Ed Wilcox took over the Lunceford band after Jimmie's death, but without much success. In this rehearsal shot, Ed is at the piano, Joe on tenor, and Omer Simeon on alto.

John Kirby

THE FIRST IMPORTANT CHAMBER JAZZ group of the Golden Age was the John Kirby Sextet. It had light, tightly scored arrangements, many of them based on "classical" themes, but it still managed to swing. Kirby's wife, popular Maxine Sullivan, became famous recording "Loch Lomond" with Claude Thornhill before joining Kirby. Some of the Kirby personnel are shown on the facing page.

(OPPOSITE) *John Kirby.*

(TOP LEFT) *William "Buster" Bailey.*

(TOP RIGHT) *Charlie Shavers.*

(MIDDLE LEFT) *Russell Procope.*

(MIDDLE RIGHT) *Maxine Sullivan.*

(LOWER LEFT) *Billy Kyle.*

THE GOLDEN AGE WAS A GOLDEN time for dozens of bands, large and small, most of them led by musicians who built a reputation while working for others, then branched out with their own groups. Here are some of those not appearing elsewhere in the book.

(OPPOSITE) Kenneth "Red" Norvo was considered by many to be the subtlest of jazz musicians. His delicate, swinging style on vibra-harp and xylophone was much admired by fellow musicians and discerning listeners. He led a series of small combos that reflected his exquisite touch.

(LEFT) Artie Shaw, with both his superb orchestra and his brilliant clarinet playing, for a while eclipsed Benny Goodman in popularity polls. A volatile artist, he kept abandoning and reentering music, finally quitting for good to become a writer. (Artie always admired writers and literature. I'll never forget the specially made "one-shelf" leather bookcase he carried around, even on one-nighters.) This shadowy portrait of him was originally used for a story that described his being half in, half out of music.

Equally volatile in his love life, Artie was married at least seven times. His wives were spectacular women and included Lana Turner, Ava Gardner, Betty Kern (Jerome Kern's daughter), and Kathleen Winsor, author of Forever Amber.

(BELOW) Charlie Barnet was a worshipful Duke Ellington fan. His band often played in the Ellington tradition and sometimes used Ellington alumni. Charlie's was the most racially integrated of the big bands. Charlie's marital history was more extravagant than Artie's; his wives weren't as famous but were even more numerous.

Woodrow "Woody" Herman had several first-rate orchestras. The first one featured the blues, a style with which his own playing and singing were most comfortable. Successive "Herman Herds" became progressively more modern.

(LEFT) Bennett "Benny" Carter was probably the most versatile of all topflight jazz musicians. He was best known for his alto sax, but he was gifted, too, on trumpet, tenor, and clarinet, besides being a superb arranger. His orchestra never received the acclaim it deserved.

(BELOW) Buddy Rich was known for his spectacular drumming and his cocky personality. I interviewed him in a theater dressing room right after one of his typically energetic performances. He was sweating and had me wait while he showered. I knew the questions I wanted to ask him but couldn't figure out how I could visually capture his feistiness with my camera. Then out of the shower he came with a leopard-spotted bathrobe. He had solved my problem!

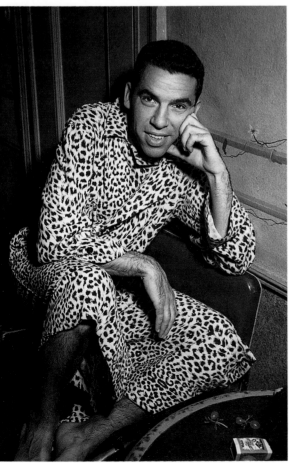

(ABOVE) Tommy Dorsey was one of the best-known orchestra leaders of the swing era. (His brother, Jimmy, had a popular band, too.) Many outstanding musicians and singers worked for him, including Frank Sinatra, who gained fame with Tommy and developed much of his singing technique by listening to Tommy's smooth, legato-style trombone. When the big band business slumped, Tommy tried a stint as a disc jockey. At his opening, he interviewed singer Beryl Davis. In the background you may be able to spot Georgie Auld, Ray McKinley, Vic Damone, Mary Lou Williams, and Josh White, all of whom were there to give his new career a boost. But to no avail. His program soon folded.

(RIGHT) Cabell "Cab" Calloway was more a novelty singer than a jazzman. (I can remember a recording date where he had a terrible time coming in on the right beat.) But he had many outstanding sidemen, all of whom got valuable exposure backing Cab's sensational personality.

Machito had a superb Latin band that was very much part of the jazz scene, with American sidemen freely intermixing with Cubans and Puerto Ricans. Here Machito (right) is playing maracas, with the rest of his rhythm section joining in.

(RIGHT) Louis Jordan and his Tympany Five was one of a number of small, good bands that specialized in novelties. The group had many smash hits, including "Knock Me a Kiss" and "Gonna Move to the Outskirts of Town." Louis was not only a witty showman but also an excellent musician; he first gained prominence as the alto star of the Chick Webb Orchestra.

(BELOW) This shot of Louis Jordan, along with one of Cab Calloway, are the exceptions to my rule never to photograph a person popping his eyes. I violated my rule only when such clowning was a significant part of a person's persona.

My policy was a problem when photographing Louis Armstrong. He knew that mugging appealed to his many audiences, and he often wanted to be photographed with eyes popping (which I wouldn't do). In the long run, his attitude proved both right and wrong: right in that some of his (to me) most grotesque photographs are more widely used than are dignified ones; wrong in that a large number of people, especially young blacks, now dismiss this greatest of instrumental geniuses as an "Uncle Tom."

(OPPOSITE) Glen "Spike" Gray, leader of the Casa Loma orchestra, had the first big white band dedicated to jazz. Its stiff arrangements kept it from being the real thing; but it came close, and its popularity, which began prior to the Golden Age, helped prepare an audience for Benny Goodman and other succeeding swing bands. (Note the target pistol on Spike's dressing table. While you're at it, compare all the discernible details in this picture with those in the picture of Duke Ellington on page 31, taken in the same dressing room from the same position.)

Nat "King" Cole with his famous trio with Oscar Moore on guitar and Johnny Miller on bass. At first Nat was primarily an instrumentalist and won polls as the country's best jazz piano player. It wasn't until later that he became a top-selling singer.

I jumped on Nat's bandwagon early—in 1940. He had a brief gig at the Silver Fox, a modest second-floor spot in downtown Washington. I had heard some of his piano records but wasn't prepared for the impact of hearing him in person. Smash! He became my favorite pianist, and he still is.

Nat Cole.

(RIGHT) Claude Thornhill was an innovator. He was the arranger and mastermind behind Maxine Sullivan's smash-hit recording of "Loch Lomond."

(BELOW) Drummer-singer Ray McKinley was the first of several men who successively took over the nominal leadership of the enormously popular Glenn Miller orchestra after Miller was lost over the English Channel while on military duty.

My first assignment after being discharged from the army was reviewing and photographing the McKinley group for Down Beat magazine. The writing part was easy. I liked what I heard and praised it. The picture part was more difficult. In my photography, I try to say something visually that augments the text; I especially try to capture personality, but Ray struck me as rather cold. I couldn't get a grip on him. Instead, I tried to suggest a drummer's motion—an idea that occurred to me because Ray was working in front of a black curtain, and I could therefore make a double exposure right in my camera.

To my delight, my inaugural efforts resulted in the magazine's cover story! Following publication, I eagerly approached Ray, expecting him to compliment me or otherwise show his appreciation. He brushed me off, and I was squashed. (I never again deliberately sought a reaction from any of my subjects.)

Forty-eight years later, I chanced to be sitting next to McKinley at a jazz party. I couldn't resist asking him about the picture. He couldn't recall it. That spurred me to get a book that contained the picture, and I showed it to him. "You took that? I've seen it hundreds of times. Bless you!" Well, it took forty-eight years, but I finally got a rise out of him.

(ABOVE) Boogie-woogie piano was a craze in the early '40s. Its most prominent artists were Meade Lux Lewis, Albert Ammons, and, shown here, Pete Johnson.

(LEFT) Dave Tough, considered by a great many musicians to be the best of the jazz drummers, was also exceptionally bright, wrote well, and could be a probing conversationalist. Despite his abilities, he was hopelessly melancholic, with a gaunt visage that matched his mournful personality.

Dave was never satisfied. Between sets on club gigs, this supreme drummer often felt obliged to go to the cellar to work out on a practice pad! That's what he was doing when this shot was taken.

(RIGHT) Belgian Jean "Toots" Thielemans created a stir in American jazz circles with his harmonica recordings. He then came to the U.S. to see what might develop. His very first day here, I introduced him to the musicians then working on 52nd Street. He felt insecure about showing up with a "mere" harmonica and carried, instead, a guitar, which was his "second" instrument. I arranged for him to sit in with Joe Marsala, whose combo was at the Hickory House. That's where this shot was taken.

Toots soon concentrated on his harmonica, and with it was very successful, especially at supplying background music for motion pictures and television programs. In the jazz magazines, he became a consistent poll winner in the "miscellaneous instrument" category. He also wrote many songs, most notably "Bluesette."

(BELOW) Bassist Bob Haggart was the key sideman of Bob Crosby's Dixieland-style orchestra. (It was a cooperative group owned by the musicians, with Bing's singing brother, Bob, chosen as the nominal leader.) While with that group, Haggart and drummer Ray Bauduc made an unconventional duet recording of a Haggart tune, "Big Noise from Winnetka;" it became an unexpected hit. Haggart composed several other songs, including "What's New" and the Dixieland anthem "South Rampart Street Parade."

Musicians in the '40s who found themselves temporarily out of work were able to keep "with it" by practicing at sessions conducted by Jacob "Brick" Fleagle, a guitarist and arranger who led a constantly changing, no-name band at Nola's rehearsal studios, on Broadway. Some days the band was a wild sight, with maybe four basses and perhaps enough brass for the gates of heaven.

In this photo Brick (at center, with hat) has several jazzmen in attendance: to his left, cornetist and close friend Rex Stewart; to Brick's right, with bow tie, trumpeter Pee Wee Erwin; and, below Pee Wee, trombonist Sandy Williams.

CLUB
SAMOA
FINK
Jimmy
RYAN'S
BAR
B.S. PULLY
CLUB CAROUSEL
HARRY the HIPSTER

Chapter 4

NEW YORK— THE CENTER OF IT ALL

Never mind New Orleans. The world center of jazz since the mid '20s has been New York City. During the Golden Age, the center of the center was a single block on 52nd Street, between Fifth and Sixth Avenues, where this photograph was taken (in 1948).

"The Street," as it was widely known, consisted of low "brownstone" buildings that had been homes for prosperous New Yorkers. By Prohibition time, the original owners had departed, and many of the ground floors and basements had been converted into speakeasies. When Prohibition laws were repealed, those premises were converted into restaurants and girlie show spots, and eventually and especially into jazz clubs.

For a decade, The Street was heaven on earth for jazz fans and jazz musicians. There were the Onyx (which was the first of the clubs), the 3 Deuces, the Downbeat, the Famous Door, Jimmy Ryan's, Kelly's Stable, and—just west of Sixth on 52nd—the Hickory House, with Birdland around the corner. The fans formed a peripatetic audience, wandering from club to club to check out a dozen living legends on any given night. Dixielanders at Ryan's. Giants like Art Tatum at the Downbeat. Gillespie and fellow boppers at the 3 Deuces. And if you were willing to stand around the bar instead of sitting at a table, you could coddle a drink costing less than a dollar and stay for an entire set, before moving on to the next piece of paradise, only a few feet away. Incidentally, this shot of 52nd Street, originally taken in color, was the construction guide for a key set in the film Bird, the Charlie Parker saga produced by Clint Eastwood.

The Street was great while it lasted. But by the end of the '40s it was dead, killed by several converging forces: an economic recession that hit the music business hard; the rise of bebop, which alienated great numbers of advocates of more traditional styles; the influx of dope peddlers and other unappetizing characters; and the inexorable encroachment of Rockefeller Center, which alone ensured The Street's demise.

Fortunately, I was there while it thrived, with an office only a few blocks away. So, in the next few pages, you'll be able to see many of the musicians, fans, and characters who were denizens of The Street.

Sitting down in a club meant a cover charge, but, of course, you got closer to the music. Here, the singer with the crutches is Doc Pomus, then an unknown blues singer who hung around the clubs for a chance to be heard. He later developed into one of the country's most successful and honored rock composers. (The accompanists that night included Sol Yaged and Rex Stewart.)

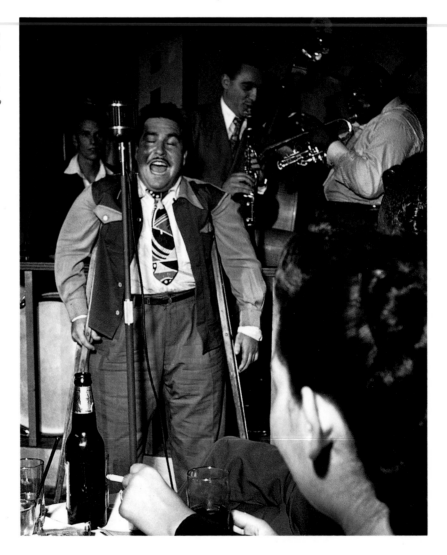

(LEFT) That's Phil Moore with the pipe. Phil was a highly regarded arranger, vocal coach, and pianist.

(BELOW) Standees crowded around a 52nd Street bar. For the price of a 75¢ drink, a fan could spend a half hour or more listening to, say, Charlie Parker.

(OPPOSITE) *Art Tatum was the piano player's piano player. Though legally blind, he covered the keyboard with awesome speed, while creating fantastic harmonic improvisations. Some critics said his prodigious embellishments destroyed the jazz feel of his music. But fellow pianists were overwhelmed. It's been said that when Tatum entered a room, some of them were known to whisper, "God is in the house."*

(LEFT) *Mary Lou Williams, the first woman to attain top-level stature in jazz, became famous as the pianist-arranger of the Andy Kirk band from Kansas City. Afterward she worked mostly with her own trio or as a single, more often in the Village than on 52nd Street.*

(BELOW) *Erroll Garner was a child prodigy who, long before he was big enough for his feet to reach the pedals, picked out tunes on his own, on the family piano. His memory was prodigious, too. This contemporary Mozart was said to have never forgotten a piece of music, once having heard it; therefore he didn't find it necessary to learn to read music— and never did. Yet he became the best-selling recording artist among jazz pianists.*

(ABOVE LEFT) *Al Hall, a sound, adaptable bassist, played everything from big band jazz to theater music and even had his own jazz record company.*

(ABOVE RIGHT) *Carl Kress, besides being an outstanding guitarist, had a special distinction: he was the co-owner of the original Onyx Club, probably the most famous of the 52nd Street jazz spots.*

(RIGHT) *William "Cozy" Cole could fit in with any style. He was a drummer for New Orleans bands, for boppers, and for everything in between.*

(LEFT) Leroy "Slam" Stewart hit it big with Slim Gaillard (Slim and Slam) on "Flat Foot Floogie." He was later part of the Art Tatum trio. Slam's playing was easily recognized: on solos, he hummed in unison with his bowing.

(RIGHT) Al Casey, shown on guitar with drummer Denzil Best and bassist John Levy, was long a mainstay with Fats Waller's combo. After Fats's death, Al worked with other small groups, usually as leader.

(BELOW) Joe Marsala, a fine clarinet and sax man, had a combo that played periodically at the Hickory House, a half-block west of the main part of The Street. His band usually included brother Marty, who was an excellent trumpet player, and Joe's wife, Adele Girard, who startled audiences with her hot harp and pretty face. I was once responsible for getting Joe's combo a gig at a new Washington club. I felt like a big shot. But Joe was paid with a rubber check and the club closed. I then felt like a jerk. However, Joe never said a word. We remained friends.

(OPPOSITE) Jean Baptiste "Django" Reinhardt, a Belgian-French Gypsy, was not one of the regular 52nd Streeters, nor—except for a brief and unsuccessful tour with Duke Ellington in 1946—was he ever personally part of the American scene. He achieved fame with his unique performances on recordings of the Quintet of the Hot Club of France. Django became the first non-American jazz giant. He is idolized by guitarists everywhere for his revolutionary technique, which he achieved despite (or maybe because of) the fact that two fingers on his fingering hand had become useless when, in his youth, his Gypsy caravan caught fire.

(OPPOSITE) Coleman "Bean" Hawkins, the greatest virtuoso of the tenor sax during the Golden Age, is one of a handful of jazz supermen. His version of "Body and Soul" became a universal jazz anthem.

(LEFT) Gene Sedric, an excellent clarinet and tenor, was for a long time the man who "ran" Fats Waller's band. Once, when Fats was too inebriated to make a scheduled appearance on an NBC/WRC show I had in Washington, Gene became a last-minute substitute and did very well. Gene was often called "Honey Bear." I could never find out why; but, for fun, I tried photographing him so that, maybe, he would look like a honey bear.

(BELOW) Sol Yaged, a symphony man turned jazzman, idolized Benny Goodman and liked to talk about him, as well as play like him. Some say he even got to look like BG. With Sol in this photo are bassist John Levy and pianist Jimmy Jones.

(OPPOSITE) Illinois Jacquet started a trend among tenor sax players with his boisterous honking on Lionel Hampton's "Flying Home." He later became a star with Jazz at the Philharmonic.

(LEFT) Bill Coleman, a sensitive, swinging horn man, was much admired by fellow musicians but found a large, appreciative audience only in France.

(BELOW) Arnett Cobb replaced Illinois Jacquet in the Hampton band, delivering frenzied Jacquet-style blowing. Here, the "World's Wildest Tenor Man" is with his own band. Arnett personally preferred playing in a warm, contemplative manner—as did Illinois. But it was better business to blow crazy.

(RIGHT) Roy "Little Jazz" Eldridge was a much-imitated trumpeter. He starred with Gene Krupa, Artie Shaw, and Fletcher Henderson, as well as with his own band. Roy was the most influential musician on his instrument between the reigns of Louis Armstrong and Dizzy Gillespie.

(BELOW) Billy Butterfield played clean, melodic trumpet much like Bobby Hackett's. He was in demand both with swing bands and with studio orchestras.

(LEFT) Hezekiah "Stuff" Smith. There are few violinists in jazz; but Stuff, using his own homemade techniques, extracted from this refined instrument a stream of witty and rollicking hot phrases. More of the same came from his pungent voice.

(BELOW) Eddie South, a classically trained musician, played a more orthodox violin than did Stuff Smith, but his fiddling nonetheless ended up . . . jazz.

(RIGHT) Bobby Hackett was the most melodic of the jazz trumpet men. When comedian Jackie Gleason chose to make records featuring "pretty" but skillfully played music, he picked Bobby to be the organizer and star of the "Gleason band."

(BELOW) Robert "Jonah" Jones, a personable trumpet player, became well known working with violinist Stuff Smith. Before he formed his own orchestra, his horn and voice were featured in various big-name bands. (The "directing" arm in this shot belongs to Cab Calloway.)

(LEFT) A jam session, with Art Hodes and Pete Johnson sharing the piano; Red Allen, trumpet; Lou McGarity, trombone; and Lester Young, with typically twisted stance, tenor sax.

(BELOW) Adrian Rollini has a niche in jazz history as the first person to swing with a bass sax. He was also one of the first to use a vibraphone.

Harlem, in upper Manhattan, was loaded with clubs, theaters, and dance halls that featured jazz. The most prominent were the Apollo Theater and the Savoy Ballroom (OPPOSITE).

Although 52nd Street was, during the Golden Age, the center of jazz in New York (and in the world), it was by no means the whole New York scene. Here are a few more New York hot spots from that period.

(LEFT) In this stunt, a wagon load of musicians rode through Times Square publicizing a jazz concert on a Hudson River sightseeing boat. Regularly, swing bands and pop singers could be heard live in the nightclubs of several hotels, like the Pennsylvania and the Astor, and on the stages of major midtown movie houses, like the Paramount and Capital Theaters. Even venerable Carnegie Hall was occasionally a venue for jazz concerts.

Chapter 5

THE VOCALISTS

The distinction between music that qualifies as jazz and that which doesn't is often subtle enough to be beyond words or metronomic measurement. The growling trumpet of Cootie Williams, for instance, is "the real thing," while the growling trumpet of Clyde McCoy is "corny." But exactly what makes them so different? It's hard to explain, though undeniably true.

Assigning vocalists to either jazz or non-jazz categories is especially difficult. What do we do with Nat Cole, an acknowledged master at the piano, who brought much of his jazz sense to his singing but used it on pop ballads and novelties? And how about Billy Eckstine, who sang a lot of schmaltz but nonetheless won the respect of most jazz musicians? Nor is it easy to explain why Mildred Bailey, with her gently swinging voice, was emphatically "in," whereas a strongly rhythmic singer like Doris Day was "out." (Did the kind of musicians with whom they associated make a difference?)

And where does this leave Frank Sinatra, who may be the finest vocalist America has produced, but who was generally ignored by the arbiters of hipness?

The author, for one, is not always sure who among the vocalists belongs in this book. Just the same, here are some of the better ones with whom I came in contact during the Golden Age, be they purveyors of 100 percent jazz or only of diluted stuff.

Billie Holiday.

(PREVIOUS SPREAD) In my picture stories, I tried to have my photographs convey qualities that went beyond what I could say with just words. In this close-up of Billie Holiday, I think I succeeded in capturing the beauty of her face and the pain in her voice. (Incidentally, an alternate take of this shot was used for a 1994 U.S. postage stamp.)

(BELOW) Billie at Carnegie Hall. This photograph was a guide for the costume in a long-running biographical play about Billie, Lady Day at Emerson's Bar & Grill. *The fingerless gloves (first popularized by the singer Hildegarde) played an especially significant, if subtle, role. At one point in the play, "Billie" feels she needs a heroin "fix" and retires temporarily from the stage. Until then, the gloves had been smoothly positioned. When she returns they are disheveled, suggesting that she slipped them aside to "shoot up." The long gloves also suggested that she had been using them all along to cover needle tracks.*

Billie Holiday

THE HAUNTING, ANGUISHED VOICE OF Billie Holiday, "Lady Day," is one of the glories of music.

Billie was a natural. While a teenager, she stunned nearly every musician who heard her heart-wrenching vocals. She was only eighteen when she made her first recording—with none less than Benny Goodman. At twenty-five, she became the featured singer with Count Basie, later with Artie Shaw. By then she also, under her own name and that of

pianist Teddy Wilson, made some of the most memorable jazz recordings of all time, using as sidemen an astounding list of instrumentalists, including Lester Young (who gave Billie the nickname Lady Day).

In 1948, Billie was at her peak, musically and physically; her splendor was, ironically, due to her having previously spent most of a year in a federal prison, serving time for possession of narcotics. Imprisoned, Billie was no longer able to obtain drugs or alcohol. As a result, she lost her previous pudginess and turned into a strikingly beautiful woman.

Her incomparable voice, instead of declining from lack of use, had actually improved.

Unable to work New York nightclubs because of restrictions on performers with criminal records, she nonetheless returned in triumph at a sold-out concert at Carnegie Hall. (That kind of venue was permitted.) Eventually, she was able to get back into clubs; it was there, as well as at Carnegie Hall, that I interviewed and photographed her.

Regrettably, Billie regressed. At the end of 1948, by which time she was again able to work the clubs, word got out that she often didn't "show" at engagements. I went, one night, anyway. Half an hour after the scheduled opening time, no Billie. Most of the audience left. I played a hunch: I snooped around the dressing rooms and found her seated, half dressed and immobile. I helped her get herself together and led her to the microphone. She looked terrible. Sounded worse. I put my notebook in my pocket, placed a lens cap on my camera, and walked out, choosing to remember this remarkable creature as she once was.

Billie with her boxer, Mister.

Ella Fitzgerald

DURING THE GOLDEN AGE, AND FOR decades thereafter, Ella Fitzgerald was the Queen of Jazz. Back in 1937, I made pilgrimages to the Savoy Ballroom in Harlem to hear the young singing sensation with the Cinderella background. When only sixteen and an orphan, she won an amateur contest, which led to her being hired as a band vocalist by Chick Webb. At twenty, with the Webb orchestra, she recorded the smash hit

"A-tisket, A-tasket" and became world famous. Her direct, solidly swinging style kept her on top year after year.

Chick was himself a phenomenon—a sickly hunchback who was one of the most dynamic drummers and leaders in jazz. In 1939, Chick died. Ella took over the band for a year, then became a single and, later, a star with *Jazz at the Philharmonic,* an enormously successful touring concert production promoted by Norman Granz.

(OPPOSITE) One night when I was present, Ella Fitzgerald dropped into a 52nd Street club that featured the Dizzy Gillespie band. She went to see her boyfriend, bassist Ray Brown. (She and Ray were later married; then, still later, divorced.) Dizzy had persuaded Ella to sing. I moved in with a camera and motioned to Dizzy to "get in the act," which he certainly did (while Ray gave him "The Eye").

In this picture, Milt Jackson can be seen off to the right. For my own amusement, I deliberately included the balding head of Timmie Rosenkrantz, a Danish nobleman and jazz fan (previously mentioned in the piece about Willie "The Lion" Smith on page 5).

Sarah "Sassy" Vaughan

SARAH VAUGHAN, "THE DIVINE SASSY," was the most prodigious of the female jazz singers. Her amazing range and adventuresome swoops and leaps were both breathtaking and musical. They made her the darling of many musicians, especially the boppers.

I caught Sassy on her first New York engagement, in a Greenwich Village club, and was suitably stunned by her skills. In her dressing room, I found her playing solitaire and photographed the event, predicting to myself that this amazing singer would not have time for solitaire for very long.

Mildred Bailey

AMONG WHITE FEMALE VOCALISTS,
the first to be hailed by the jazz cognoscenti
was Mildred Bailey (actually, she was part
Native American). Mildred, a big woman with
a delicate voice, had an exquisite sense of timing. Her singing may have been quiet, but it
created a real jazz beat. Mildred was married
to xylophonist Red Norvo and, for a while,
jointly led an orchestra with him. (One of my
shots of her was the model for a U.S. postage
stamp in 1994.)

June Christy

ONE OF THE MOST POPULAR OF THE
good band vocalists was June Christy,
featured for years with the Stan Kenton
orchestra. Compared to, say, Mildred Bailey,
hers was a husky, driving voice. She was in a
groove first developed by Anita O'Day.

(LEFT) Mildred Bailey.
(ABOVE) June Christy.

(BELOW LEFT) *Sylvia Syms.*

(BELOW RIGHT) *Ethel Waters.*

(OPPOSITE) *Dardanelle.*

Sylvia Syms

THERE WERE MANY OTHER FINE FEMALE singers in the Golden Age. One was Sylvia Syms, whose voice was frequently compared to that of her idol, Billie Holiday. (It was Sylvia who told Billie to use gardenias in her hair—to cover a temporarily scorched area. It became something of a Holiday trademark.)

Ethel Waters

ETHEL WATERS HAD, BY THE '40S, become a popular actress who, when she sang at all, used very little jazz. Earlier, however, she was a successful blues singer who was accompanied by leading jazzmen and who inspired many young black performers.

Dardanelle

DARDANELLE (JUST DARDANELLE) WAS another singer who was compared to the established greats. She was a young southerner with the proper manners of an elderly Dixie dowager. But she swung mightily not only with her voice but on piano and vibraphone.

Lena Horne

LENA HORNE WAS GENERALLY not classified as a jazz singer, but she had an expressive voice, was a commendable actress and entertainer, and was gorgeous to look at—a combination that made her a star.

Doris Day

DORIS DAY AND HER LONGTIME BOSS, Les Brown, were not deeply into jazz, but their beat was sound and the music swung. Doris later left the band business for the movies and became for several years the leading female box office draw in Hollywood.

(BELOW LEFT) *Jimmy Rushing.*

(BELOW RIGHT & OPPOSITE) *Mel Tormé.*

Jimmy Rushing

MANY OF THE BEST MALE VOCALISTS were blues singers, such as Leadbelly and Big Joe Turner. Another was Jimmy Rushing (whose rotund configuration earned him the appellation "Mr. Five-by-Five"—five feet tall and five feet wide). Jimmy was one of the few bluesmen attached to an orchestra; for years, he was a star of the Count Basie band. (This shot of Jimmy, as with my portraits of Billie Holiday and Mildred Bailey, was used in the preparation of a 1994 U.S. postage stamp.)

Mel Tormé

PROBABLY THE MOST SKILLFUL MALE singer on the jazz scene has been Mel Tormé. He began his career as a drummer and brought thorough musical control and intelligence to his role as a vocalist. Mel has been able to pull off imaginative creations no other singer dared even attempt. Additionally, Mel was an actor, author, and arranger, as well as the composer of such hits as "The Christmas Song" ("Chestnuts Roasting on an Open Fire"), the perennial favorite first made famous by Nat Cole.

Because of his hoarse yet smoothly hushed vocal quality, he was, early on, appropriately called "The Velvet Fog." One day, while in his theater dressing room waiting for him to prepare for a performance, I got an idea about how to "visualize" his foggy voice. I ran out to the nearest delicatessen, bought some dry ice, and dumped it into his dressing room sink. I then had him get to the side of the sink, and after turning on the water to form dry ice clouds, had him sing, with the result you see below.

(BELOW) Jack Teagarden.

(OPPOSITE TOP) Joe Mooney at accordion with Gaeton "Gate" Frega (left) at bass and Andy Fitzgerald (right), clarinet.

(OPPOSITE BOTTOM, LEFT TO RIGHT) Louis Armstrong, Nat "King" Cole, Roy Eldridge.

MOST OF THE OUTSTANDING MALE JAZZ vocalists were instrumentalists who adapted their horn and keyboard phrasing to their singing. Pictures of many of the instrumentalist-singers appear elsewhere in this book. Louis Armstrong, who is preeminent among them, also appears here, as do several other outstanding examples of the genre: Jack Teagarden, Joe Mooney, Nat Cole, and Roy Eldridge.

Nat Cole

OF ALL THE INSTRUMENTALISTS WHO turned to singing, Nat Cole gained the greatest popular success. The fantastic reception given to such Cole records as "The Christmas Song" and "Nature Boy" led to his minimizing the piano. He concentrated instead on pop vocals, complete with lush string backgrounds; but his jazz-based style gave distinction to the most maudlin material.

Joe Mooney

FOR ME, THE MOST UNDERRATED all-around jazzman of the period was Joe Mooney. Joe, who was blind, could sing like a hip angel, write arrangements suitable for a heavenly combo, play the piano and organ divinely, and—most wonderful of all—squeeze jazz from an accordion, which is a miracle only slightly less wonderful than squeezing blood from a stone.

Joe paid his dues over the years by working for big bands in one or another of his several identities. Then in 1946 he formed a quartet, with himself handling the accordion and the vocals. The group was soon hailed by Mike Levin of *Down Beat* as "The most exciting musical unit in the U.S. today. . . . [Joe] is the best male vocalist on the scene." With Mike's stupendous push, Joe quickly got choice club dates and a record contract. His quartet rocketed heavenward, where it belonged, only to fizzle and plunge back to earth, all in a matter of months. The quartet broke up, with one sideman retiring into a religious order.

Joe's problem was that his music was too quiet, too subtle. His suspenseful timing and sensitive inflections made his music jump like mad. But you had to listen. Carefully. And too few bothered.

(BELOW) Dave Lambert (at left) leading the Pastels, a group that sang with Stan Kenton.

SCAT SINGING IS THE USE BY SINGERS of nonsense syllables instead of words, with the syllables phrased as if coming from a jazz horn. Louis Armstrong was supposed to have invented scat when he forgot the lyrics of a song during a recording session.

During the '40s, scatting became widespread. Louis continued to lead the way; Ella, Leo Watson, and others followed. Some singers made scatting their specialty. The most intriguing of them was Babs Gonzales, who scatted in a bop groove. He was a composer, too. His biggest composition: "Oo-pa-pa-da."

Dave Lambert, a director of vocal groups and himself a singer, extended the use of voices-as-horns. He used actual words, as well as nonsense syllables, to produce the effects of a bop combo.

It's frequently difficult to decide which performer goes in what chapter of this book, and that's certainly true of Dave, Babs, June, Sarah, and many others, for they are not only singers but also part of the modern jazz world. Keep them in mind as you read Chapter Seven: "Bop . . . and All That Modern Jazz!"

Quite the opposite of scat singers was Billy Eckstine, whose incredibly rich baritone delivered straightforward, romantic lyrics.

Babs Gonzales.

Billy Eckstine.

Frank Sinatra

FRANK SINATRA WAS SNUBBED BY MANY serious jazz fans, but they were wrong. The skinny kid who set the world on its ear when he sang with the Tommy Dorsey band always sang with an impeccably swinging beat, and, when it was appropriate, he sang pure jazz.

Frank was a master at projection. With his skillful use of microphones, his flawless diction, and his ability to impart the meaning of the lyrics in a song, he was able to make each individual in an auditorium of thousands feel as if Frank were singing just to him or, especially, to her.

In a way, Frank had a negative effect on jazz and the Golden Age; he, more than any other individual, brought about the decline of the big swing bands, which for years had stimulated all of jazz music. An economic slump had already doomed large groups. It was Frank who delivered the coup de grace by making singers more important than orchestras. No longer merely vocalists who augmented the music of the bands, singers became the main attractions, with orchestras reduced to accompanists or consigned to oblivion.

Chapter 6

BEFORE & BEHIND THE GOLDEN AGE

The Golden Age of Jazz began in the middle 1930s. But it didn't spring out of nowhere. Armstrong and Ellington were playing it earlier. So was Fletcher Henderson, who, in the early '20s, led orchestras consisting of talents like Rex Stewart, Benny Carter, Roy Eldridge, Sid Catlett, and Armstrong himself. The Ben Pollack band had Glenn Miller, Harry James, and Benny Goodman (long before Benny sparked the Golden Age). About the same time that Pollack's groups performed, there was the highly successful Red Nichols and his Five Pennies; at one time or another, the Pennies included Jimmy Dorsey, Joe Venuti, and (again) Glenn Miller and Benny Goodman.

Many others, some going back to the turn of the century, played hot music: King Oliver, Bunk Johnson, Bix Beiderbecke, Don Redman, Bennie Moten, Kid Ory, Scott Joplin, Jelly Roll Morton, Sidney Bechet, The Original Dixieland Jazz Band, and hundreds more.

I, of course, was able to interview and photograph only some of the pioneers. Many appear elsewhere in this book. Here are three more that deserve attention: Paul Whiteman, Red McKenzie, and Gene Goldkette.

Paul Whiteman.

(PREVIOUS SPREAD) *Through the '20s and much of the '30s, Paul Whiteman was known everywhere as "the King of Jazz." He was indeed an important and regal personage, but the jazz title was a press agent's fabrication. His orchestra's jazz was minimal, though its members did include noted "hot" musicians like Bix Beiderbecke, Red Norvo, and the Dorsey brothers, whose jazz expressions occasionally penetrated through Whiteman's symphonic arrangements. (In this photograph you see Whiteman listening to the Joe Mooney Quartet.)*

(RIGHT) *William "Red" McKenzie was a singer who led a Condon-type jazz group called the Mound City Blues Blowers. Besides singing, he blew blues on a comb covered with tissue paper, which made a sound like a kazoo. It sold a lot of records!*

(BELOW) *Much like the Whiteman orchestra, Gene Goldkette's band was big, successful, and employed many of the same musicians: Beiderbecke, the Dorseys, and others. They had considerable freedom to do their thing, making Goldkette a significant element in jazz history.*

MANY PEOPLE WERE BEHIND THE SCENES, making the Golden Age possible. Probably the most important was John Hammond, who played a crucial role in the careers of a dozen outstanding performers, from Bessie Smith and Billie Holiday to Benny Goodman and Count Basie. (More details about Hammond can be found in the section on Benny Goodman in Chapter Three.) John was a friend of mine, but I never had an assignment to interview or photograph him. Too bad.

I also missed out on Leonard Feather, who was the leading jazz journalist. But I did catch other nonmusicians who had critical roles.

Norman Granz was a fabulous promoter of jazz concerts. His Jazz at the Philharmonic *tours, featuring greats like Ella Fitzgerald and Oscar Peterson, gave jazz a tremendous boost at a time when it was at a low point. His exemplary treatment of the performers and his insistence that audiences not be segregated gave him high marks in the music industry. Granz, in addition to his concert promotions, created several record labels.*

(RIGHT) *Hugues Panassie with one of his very favorite musicians, guitarist Tiny Grimes.*

(BELOW) *Charles Delaunay (at left).*

IN THE MIDDLE '30S, JAZZ RECEIVED unusual attention with the publication of two epochal books, both by Frenchmen: *Le Jazz Hot* by Hugues Panassie and *Hot Discography* by Charles Delaunay. The former, a serious discourse on hot music, strongly favored New Orleans jazz and its associated styles. The latter was the first major effort to list great numbers of jazz recordings, complete with dates and personnel—an achievement Delaunay was able to accomplish without getting to the U.S., where most of the recordings were made.

Delaunay, the son of two famous painters, Robert and Sonia, finally got to America and stayed with me for several days. In the picture to the left, he's visiting 52nd Street with Walter Schaap, his American representative and editor. (Walter later joined my company when I left jazz to become a producer of educational filmstrips. His son, Phil, not yet born at the time, has become one of the nation's outstanding jazz broadcasters and historians. This book is dedicated to Walter and Phil.)

The Commodore Record Shop on 42nd Street, run by Milt Gabler, was the first important store to specialize in jazz records. It also was the first small, independent producer of jazz recordings; its output included such memorable sides as Billie Holiday's "Strange Fruit." In this picture, Milt is at left. The salesman at right is Jack Crystal, Milt's brother-in-law and the father of the actor-comedian-to-be, Billy Crystal.

Ahmet and Nesuhi Ertegun.

MANY OF TODAY'S RECORD COMPANIES were started by people who loved jazz. Such was clearly the case with Ahmet and Nesuhi Ertegun, who were smitten by the music while living in Europe, where their father was filling various high-level positions for the Turkish government. When their father became the Turkish ambassador to the United States, the Ertegun brothers were in their element. In Washington, they began promoting jazz concerts and getting involved in other activities, including appearances in my *Washington Post* music column and on my NBC/WRC radio show.

After their father died, the brothers chose to remain in America. Ahmet eventually became the primary founder of Atlantic Records, and Nesuhi eventually became head of the foreign operations of WEA (Warner/Electra/Atlantic).

A personal note: Nesuhi and I twice played in the National Table Tennis Doubles Championships. (We practiced on a table in the Turkish Embassy's huge ballroom.)

(LEFT) *Johnny Mercer was a jazz singer with Whiteman, Goodman, and others. More significantly, he was a founder of Capitol Records and the composer or lyricist of many popular songs, including "Laura," "Skylark," "That Old Black Magic," and "Come Rain or Come Shine."*

(BELOW) *I did stories on Leonard Bernstein because though he was primarily an outstanding conductor, pianist, composer, and lecturer, all in classical music, he also gave much support to jazz and composed the musical comedies* West Side Story *and* On the Town. *In audacious moments, this incredible polymath even tried playing jazz with an entire symphony orchestra. He shouldn't have.*

No sooner had big band swing established its sovereignty than dissidents revolted against it. As early as 1940 they condemned as sterile almost every cherished standard established during a half-century of jazz evolution. Why must there be the same old theme-with-variations format? they asked. Why must jazz be danceable? Why must it be entertaining? Melodious? Harmonious? Why stick to either two-four time or four-four time? Why not five-four? Or any other regular beat? Or no regular beat?

Nothing was sacred.

The revolutionaries formed two different groups, each with its own musical alternatives. The major group was, at least in its origins, entirely black; and its ideas, though radically new, were homegrown. If modern European "classical" concepts were at all worked into its sounds, this was done subconsciously.

The music of this group was called bebop, later abbreviated to bop. At first hearing, bop jarred listeners; they were unprepared for the onslaught. Bop was also devilishly difficult to play, with eccentric starts and stops, torrents of notes played at machine-gun tempos, and seemingly undisciplined solos relieved by rapid-fire unison choruses. This was jazz? Few of the established musicians thought so. Even fewer could play it.

The bop movement was a creation of the young—people in their teens and early twenties, like Kenny Clarke, Charlie Christian, Ken Kersey, Oscar Pettiford, and the three dominant personalities: Charlie Parker, Dizzy Gillespie, and Thelonious Monk. Bird was generally regarded as the intuitive genius and improviser of the group; Diz, the conscious thinker and showman; and Monk, the clearinghouse and refiner.

Chapter 7

BOP! . . . AND ALL THAT MODERN JAZZ

Thelonious Monk.

BY THE LATE 1940S, WHEN BIG BAND swing had declined, bop had matured and begun to dominate the jazz scene. Commercially, and perhaps artistically, that scene was not nearly what it once had been. But the revolution did, in a sense, succeed.

The boppers' revolution was more than a musical upheaval. It was social as well. James Lincoln Collier, in his penetrating history *The Making of Jazz,* points out that the black men who created bop deliberately turned the old ways upside down in order to show their independence. Further, the modern black musician often acquired "cool" habits of language, dress, and behavior to help reinforce the impression that he was now an artist and no longer a mere entertainer: "He eschewed anything that smacked of emotionalism. Not for him the grin and widespread arms of Armstrong; instead he coolly bowed to his audience at the end of a number and walked offstage."

The second revolutionary group—sometimes allied to but still quite different from the boppers—consisted mostly of whites. Its music, sometimes tagged "progressive jazz," deliberately incorporated the principles and devices of modern European "classical" music. The leaders included Stan Kenton, Dave Brubeck, Lennie Tristano, John Lewis (of the Modern Jazz Quartet), Woody Herman, Boyd Raeburn, and Claude Thornhill, though each was sufficiently different from the others so that they would probably have objected to my making them bedfellows.

Many critics felt that progressive jazz wasn't jazz at all, that it didn't swing, which was sometimes said about bop, too. Some modernists denied that their music didn't swing; others responded by asking: "Who says it has to?"

Whatever bop and progressive jazz may not have been, they definitely were the most vital forms of music to be found during the last years of the Golden Age.

Thelonious Sphere Monk

SOME TIME IN AUGUST 1947 IT OCCURRED to me that whereas Dizzy, Bird, and Thelonious were the most talked-about musicians of the day, only the first two were identities you could put your finger on. Dizzy was everywhere: the ubiquitous General of bop leading his various troops. Bird, well, when he wasn't in a hospital, he was playing club dates; either way, you knew where he was. But what about Thelonious? No one I knew had seen him for nearly a year. Was he working somewhere? Sick? Was he even alive? Finding Thelonious became my special mission.

I found his mother's phone number and called. But she hadn't seen her boy for half a year. I located the last place he was known to have worked. But the manager said that ten months earlier Thelonious had gone out for a smoke during an intermission, and had yet to return.

There was more of the same until I happened to mention my problem to Mary Lou Williams. Mary Lou, besides being a great piano player, was the focal point for musicians who wanted to keep up with what was happening. Jazz people were constantly dropping in at her apartment. It was a salon.

Mary Lou was just the person to provide a solution to my quest. "You want Thelonious? You'll get Thelonious." She rubbed her magic lantern and sure enough, within a week Thelonious, very shy, showed up at my Rockefeller Center office.

Unfortunately, the setting unnerved Monk, and my interview floundered. So we shifted, via taxi, to Minton's Playhouse, an undistinguished-looking night club in Harlem. It was at Minton's that bop had actually been incubated some six or seven years earlier. (Probably never before in history had a complete art movement been created in a single room.)

Once Thelonious felt relaxed, he proved to be articulate and informative. He told me that the club had been founded by Henry

Minton, the first black delegate to Local 802 of the musicians' union, and that Teddy Hill, a former swing band leader, took over the management of the club in 1940. Though Teddy's own tastes were conservative, he encouraged the most iconoclastic musicians to drop in and jam, even providing them with free food on Mondays (when musicians with jobs had the night off). Teddy figured that if the hippest musicians made Minton's their hangout, paying customers would come to listen. He was right, so he kept the place congenial to musicians with experimental proclivities. Before long, even the top white jazzmen showed up to find out what was new, and to join in the jam sessions. Supposedly,

Thelonious Monk at Minton's piano.

some of the trickiest and most radical inventions in bop were deliberately developed by Minton's black regulars just to frustrate the visiting big-name whites and keep them, with their big reputations, from dominating the Monday night sessions.

In any case, Minton's prospered and the new music burgeoned. Suddenly Teddy Hill found himself the guardian angel of bop.

At Minton's, Thelonious had acted as a kind of house pianist and resident composer. He was also the respected guru to whom visiting musicians came with their latest ideas, to have them appraised and refined. Pianos are well suited for working on musical problems, so it was largely around Monk and his piano that the new music developed. I photographed Thelonious playing on the very instrument where it had all happened.

During my conversation with Thelonious, trumpeter Howard McGhee dropped around, then trumpeter Roy Eldridge and manager Teddy Hill. Howard got Monk to dream up some horn passages and then persuaded him to write them down on score sheets. That's one of the ways musicians made use of Monk's overflowing creative talents.

Teddy Hill pulled me aside and spoke about Thelonious. "He's the guy who deserves the most credit for creating bop. I know. I was there."

I never did find out where Monk had been through the previous months, but Teddy indirectly explained Thelonious's mysterious ways. "He's completely absorbed in thinking about music. Maybe he's on the way to meet you. An idea comes to him. He begins to work on it. Mop! Days go by and he's still at it. He's forgotten all about you and everything else but that idea."

Soon after the session at Minton's, I placed illustrated articles on Monk in *Down Beat,* the *Record Changer,* and the *Saturday Review.* As a result of the publicity, Thelonious was offered several gigs. He was once again back on the music scene, and there he stayed—more or less. The one time I went to see Monk at work, he didn't quite recognize me. It didn't matter. I had accomplished what I had set out to do. I had found Thelonious Sphere Monk.

(LEFT) Mary Lou Williams's "salon." At this particular gathering, Mary Lou is seated, center. From the left: Dizzy Gillespie, pianist-arranger Tadd Dameron, pianist Hank Jones. At far right: trombonist Jack Teagarden.

(BELOW) Thelonious Monk with Howard McGhee, Roy Eldridge, and Teddy Hill.

Charles "Yardbird" Parker

BIRD WAS WIDELY ACKNOWLEDGED
to be the supreme jazz genius of his time. He
was also widely acknowledged to be the most
self-destructive. Drugs. Alcohol. You name it.
But somehow his musical talents prevailed
over his worst excesses. When he was blowing, Bird could effortlessly produce chorus
after chorus of wondrous improvisations.
He could turn standard tunes into amazing
melodies no one had ever heard before.

These photos of Bird were taken soon
after he returned East from a long stay in
Camarillo, a California hospital where he had
recovered from a major breakdown. Despite
a strange look in his eyes, he never was
healthier or more relaxed. But, in time, he
again pushed the self-destruct button. Bird
slowly fell apart and died at age thirty-five.
Significantly, the attending physician took
him to be a man in his mid-fifties.

*(LEFT) Charlie Parker with bassist
Tommy Potter.*

*(BELOW) Bird with his ardent
disciple, trumpeter Robert "Red"
Rodney. In the mirror: Dizzy
Gillespie and Clyde Lombardi.*
  *Rodney virtually clung to his
idol. His attachment to Parker is
shown in the biographical motion
picture* Bird. *In one scene in the
movie, Red tries to join the Parker
combo on a tour of the Deep South.
He's turned down; a white musician in a black orchestra would
have been dangerous. Red persists,
and a solution is found: he is passed
off as a black albino—Albino Red,
blues singer and trumpet sensation! Or so it said in the movie.*

John Birks "Dizzy" Gillespie

YOU'D THINK FROM HIS NICKNAME
and his onstage antics that Dizzy Gillespie was
the wildest of the many wild bop musicians.
Not so. He was, on the contrary, practical-
minded, singularly dependable, and intelligent.

Not that he didn't deserve the name Dizzy.
But that went back to his exuberant younger
days. There was the much-repeated story
involving, of all things, a spitball that someone threw while the Cab Calloway band was
performing in a theater. In the ensuing argu-
ment Diz nicked Cab with a knife.

Or there were the frantic times when an
even younger Gillespie worked for Teddy
Hill. Teddy once gave me some details:
"Right off, at his first rehearsal, he began to
play in an overcoat, hat, and gloves. For a
while, everyone was set against this maniac.
Me, too. I gave him the name 'Dizzy.'

"When I took my band to Europe, some
of the guys threatened not to go if the crazy
one went, too. But by then I realized that,
with all his eccentricities and practical jokes,
he was the most stable of us all. Sure enough,
he turned out to be the one with the cleanest
habits and the best business sense. He saved
so much money in Europe that he encouraged the others to borrow from him, just so
he'd have an income in case things got rough
back in the States: Diz crazy? Diz was crazy
like a fox."

It was almost a sacred obligation for modern musicians to be cool. But Diz couldn't
contain his antic spirits. He hammed up his
performances as much as did Armstrong
before him. And whereas some modern-jazz
theologians advocated austere banker's-gray
suits, Diz made a uniform out of a beret,
heavy-rimmed glasses, and a Vandyke beard.
Hundreds of other boppers emulated him.

Diz's original contributions went beyond
things sartorial. He showed that bop, which
started as music for small combos, would
work successfully with big bands. He then

*Here's Dizzy's battle regalia in
1948. The now-famous uptilted
horn came later. (When I supplied
the cover for Dizzy's autobiography,*
To Be Or Not to Bop, *I started
with the above photo caricature,
then cheated by slicing off the bell of
the trumpet and pasting it back on
in a tilted position.)*

showed that there was a place in jazz orchestras for Afro-Cuban rhythms. And, above all, he showed that a trumpet could be used in remarkable new ways.

Diz's playing was incredible: gushes of extremely rapid notes, each cleanly articulated, and the whole of it making good jazz sense instead of being a mere display of virtuosity. And leave it to Diz to do it in his own peculiar way. A trumpet player's lips and tongue and cheeks—his embouchure—is supposed to be held in, tightly. But Dizzy

puffed his cheeks like balloons. And that neck! On the strong notes, it bulged until it actually looked as if it would burst. Everything was wrong with his playing, except the result.

It was inevitable that Diz, the colorful yet dependable genius, would assume the leadership of the bop movement. This he did with confidence and flair. And when bop took over 52nd Street toward the end of the '40s, Diz just naturally became King of The Street.

This big band included John Lewis, piano (later the founder of the Modern Jazz Quartet); Ray Brown, bass; Cecil Payne, baritone; James Moody, tenor; Howard Johnson, alto; Miles Davis, trumpet (hidden in the rear shadows); and Duke Ellington (painted on Dizzy's tie).

(LEFT) *Dizzy Gillespie, King of The Street.*

(BELOW) *Diz at full blast: cheeks ballooning, neck bulging.*

Stan Kenton

STAN KENTON WAS ONE OF THE MOST prominent of those modern jazzmen whose music was consciously influenced by "classical" forms. Stan had at least one other distinction: he was the most controversial of the modern music makers.

Those who couldn't stand his orchestra found it pretentious, devoid of swing, and just plain awful. Yet such denigrations could, at worst, characterize only his more formal concert pieces. Most of his music over the years did swing—enough so that his orchestra was voted best swing band of the year in the *Down Beat* polls of 1947, 1950, 1951, 1952, 1953, and 1954.

It is a fact that his music, which he called "progressive jazz," often favored tightly written scores over improvisation, mixed tempos within a single tune, and used still other characteristics associated more with European music than with American jazz. In particular, he was not beholden to the big beat. "It's not the rhythm that counts," he would say, "it's the personalized warmth." But was his music warm? His numerous detractors protested that it was absolutely cold.

Warm or cold, it was loud. Stan's screaming horns presaged the high decibels of the rock age, but his stalwarts did it without electronic amplification. Just old-fashioned lung power. When Stan raised his long arms to call for "more," the men in the brass section blew until their faces reddened, their eyes bulged, and incipient hernias popped.

I once spent nearly a week with Stan and his orchestra doing one-nighters. One-nighters were—and probably still are—a remunerative but baneful part of every "name" orchestra's existence. They meant traveling hundreds of miles a day, day after day for weeks, playing a dance here on one night, a concert there on the next night, and

so on, the fees and distances depending on the popularity of the band and the skills of the band's booking agent.

One-nighters could turn into a rigorous, wearisome regimen for the musicians of any orchestra. It was even tougher for the members of the Kenton band, for Stan was a perfectionist driven by two inextricably connected forces: a desire for personal success and a crusade for progressive jazz.

Typically, the band would play, say, a concert, ending at eleven p.m. Stan would give the group a short break, but get it back for a strenuous rehearsal lasting an hour or so. Only then were the musicians released. Generally, they'd go—where else?—to a local music spot for a late snack and to hear what the local cats were blowing.

Then to their hotel. Late to bed. Late to rise. After breakfast, musicians and wives into bus. Instruments into truck. Next town, maybe 150 miles away. Where's Stan? Up early. Raced ahead in own car, like the wind (me along, a little scared). Interview with reporter. Visit to college music department. Session with one, two local disc jockeys. Stan very bright. Very persuasive. By now, gang has arrived. Check in at hotel. Time and weather permitting, a quick game of intraband baseball. But not for Stan. He's phoning ahead. Interviews to set for tomorrow, 200 miles away. Now it's concert time. Or dance time. Then it starts all over again.

Some days are a little different. Like that night we went to a club and got talking to a trio of college students, a little drunk, who made it clear they didn't like Kenton's music. I left the club a minute after the rest. Seeing me leave alone and thinking I was part of the band, the trio jumped me. I yelled. Eddie Safranski, an average-sized fellow made husky by wrestling a bass, rushed in like a squad of marines. Very gutsy. End of students.

A week to remember.

(RIGHT) In the Golden Age, running a big, successful band was like running a big business, and that was certainly true of the Kenton orchestra. It required a large staff, besides the musicians. Stan met frequently with his staff. The fellow seated at the right is Carlos Gastel, Stan's personal manager. (Other Gastel clients included Nat Cole, Mel Tormé, and Peggy Lee.) Also at the session are the orchestra's publicity person, a booking agent, an advance man, a road manager (in this case, Bob Gioga, who doubled on baritone sax and is seated next to Stan); and an office manager.

(BELOW) A big bus was necessary. Kenton also had a large truck to hold instruments and two band boys to handle the stuff. Stan, himself, drove his own car so that he could rush ahead to the next venue, to be interviewed by the media, while his musicians slept.

(OPPOSITE) Stan drove his musicians hard. Here, after an hour break following a concert, he's holding a rehearsal with the help of his principal arrangers, Pete Rugolo (left) and Bob Graettinger.

Stan was a tough boss but a considerate one. He encouraged his musicians to have their spouses and young children join them on road trips.

To break the monotony of long trips—of which there were many— the Kentonites carried everything from playing cards to catcher's masks.

(RIGHT) The Kenton orchestra had many stars, each widely known. Shelly Manne was one of the most famous. He went on to lead small combos.

(BELOW) Sometimes the audiences were predominantly male, which is certainly the case with the crowd that's grouped around June Christy.

This is one of my favorite "story-telling" pictures. Examine the faces. What is the young man thinking as he stares at June? What is his date thinking? And what about the young lady at the right?

(OPPOSITE) During the Golden Age, dances could be more like concerts. The "dancers," a great many without partners, stood as close as they could to their favorite musicians. The idol here is Eddie Safranski.

Stan Kenton was an intense, driven man with two goals: one was personal success; the other, inseparable from the first, was making *his* kind of jazz, progressive jazz, the music of the future. He was not successful. Bop and its even more modern variants seem to have fared better. But his influence has continued strong in high school and college orchestras and in academic courses. For a long time, he sought extended visits to colleges, where, in addition to playing concerts, he held clinics. Perhaps the Kenton approach does better in schools because, like classical music, it can be more readily "written down" and performed as written.

Laurindo Almeida was a classical concert musician who added Latin flavor to the band. Stan, along with Dizzy Gillespie, was one of the first to blend Latin colors with jazz.

Kenton, like Ellington, had an especially strong trombone section. Two of its principals were Eddie Bert (ABOVE) and Kai Winding (MIDDLE).

(BELOW) Kenton's music, frequently loud and discordant, was often called "shattering." Backstage at a Richmond, Virginia, theater, I tried portraying this quality by photographing the reflections of Stan and Buddy Childers in a broken mirror.

THE TWO GROUPS OF MODERNISTS—
the boppers and progressives—were not always easily differentiated. Some of their members straddled both camps. Others kept one foot planted in early forms of jazz. The next few pages display photos of some of those musicians who were identified with modern jazz, whatever their specific cubicle might have been.

(RIGHT) Max Roach was the greatest of the bop drummers.

(BELOW) Theodore "Fats" Navarro, trumpet, died at twenty-six—a tragic genius in the Charlie Parker mold. Tadley "Tadd" Dameron, seated at center, was probably bopland's favorite arranger. The tenor is Charles Rouse; the alto, Ernie Henry.

(OPPOSITE) Fats Navarro.

Allen Eager, a devotee of Lester Young's playing style, was closely associated with Tadd and Fats, as well as with several swing bands. With him here are drummer Art Mardigan and bassist Curly Russell.

(LEFT) *Bill De Arango was a modern guitarist with outstanding technical skills. Terry Gibbs was, along with Milt Jackson, the top young vibes artist of the era.*

(BELOW) *Barbara Carroll, pianist, was probably the first female bop musician. For a while she led a trio that featured guitarist Chuck Wayne and bassist Clyde Lombardi.*

(OPPOSITE) Billy Taylor, a remarkably versatile jazz figure, played with top swing, Latin, and bop combos, eventually developing a smooth, moderately bop style. Holder of a Ph.D. degree, Taylor also had roles as a lecturer on jazz and a producer of jazz programs.

(LEFT) Boniface "Buddy" De Franco was one of the few modernists on the clarinet, an instrument that greatly declined in popularity by the late '40s. Here he's working on the portable piano he carried on trips, while his wife organizes their clothes.

(BELOW LEFT) Milton "Bags" Jackson. His vibraharp was the dominant voice of the Modern Jazz Quartet. The bassist in this photo is Ray Brown.

(BELOW RIGHT) Billy "Mr. B" Eckstine, best known as a singer, led an orchestra that, at various times, included Charlie Parker, Sarah Vaughan, Dizzy Gillespie, Fats Navarro, Miles Davis, Art Blakey, Tadd Dameron, Lucky Thompson, and Dexter Gordon.

(RIGHT) Georgie Auld moved progressively from swing to modern music. Here he's leading a combo that featured several illustrious boppers. At left is Serge Chaloff, on baritone; on trumpet, Red Rodney; on drums, Norman "Tiny" Kahn.

(BELOW) Joseph "Flip" Phillips, known for his crowd-rousing tenor, is shown fronting an all-star combo consisting of Bill Harris, trombone, a giant at his instrument; Denzil Best, drums, long a key man with the Shearing Quintet; Billy Bauer, guitar, a frequent poll winner; Greig "Chubby" Jackson, bass, the popular dynamo of many rhythm sections; and Lennie Tristano, piano, who was one of the most distinctive modern theorists and the leader of a musically radical cult.

(FAR LEFT) Here's a remarkable lineup of most of the top progressive-jazz arrangers. From the top: Eddie Sauter, Ed Finckel, George Handy, Johnny Richards, Neal Hefti, and Ralph Burns.

(LEFT & BELOW LEFT) Boyd Raeburn led the farthest-out progressive band of the period. He had the support of Duke Ellington; and at one time or another, his sidemen included Dizzy Gillespie and Buddy De Franco, as well as arrangers Ed Finckel, George Handy, and Johnny Richards. He was married to his singer, Ginnie Powell, shown studying a chart during a rehearsal. (Their son, Bruce, became curator of the Hogan Jazz Archive at Tulane University.)

(OPPOSITE) Woody Herman had several "Herds" and used several separate styles. During one period he went heavily into progressive, European-oriented music. Igor Stravinsky wrote "Ebony Concerto" for him. Shown here at a rehearsal are Walter Hendl of the National Symphony Orchestra, who conducted the premiere of the concerto; Tony Aless, piano; Billy Bauer, guitar; Chubby Jackson, bass; Don Lamond, drums; Woody Herman, clarinet; Flip Phillips, tenor.

(LEFT) Charlie Ventura made his name as a tenor saxophonist with Gene Krupa, then led a number of exciting combos. He shared the leadership of one group with trombonist Bill Harris (right).

(BELOW) The unusual orchestra of Claude Thornhill included French horns and other exotic instruments. Many of the musicians were prominent jazzmen. Danny Polo is at the rear, second from left; Lee Konitz, one of Tristano's leading disciples, third from left. Other Thornhill jazzmen were Gerry Mulligan and Gil Evans, neither one shown here.

Miles Davis

MILES DAVIS WAS THE LAST STAR of the Golden Age of Jazz—the perfect person with whom to conclude this book.

Let me go back to a day in 1947 when I went to Nola's rehearsal studio on Broadway, to cover a new band that bop trumpeter Howard McGhee was rehearsing. After taking notes for my story, I shot a few photographs, one of which showed an unknown, handsome, well-dressed young man with intense, piercing eyes that zeroed in on Howard. I was told that the onlooker was a kid from Juilliard, the music school. I didn't get his name and never used the picture, preferring another one.

More than thirty years later, while going through my files, I suddenly recognized "the kid." It was Miles Davis.

By the time Miles was twenty-one, it was impossible not to recognize him. He had become the most sought-after of musicians. When Coleman Hawkins, an elder jazz giant, probed the new sounds, he hired Miles as his trumpet man. When Charlie Parker could no longer get Dizzy to play with him, he got Miles. When Diz himself built a big band, he chose Miles to back him up. And when Gerry Mulligan, Gil Evans, and other Thornhill alumni were looking for an inspired trumpet to lead their new group in a recording that would launch "cool jazz," they, too, turned to Miles.

The career of Miles Davis kept rising, into years beyond the scope of this book; but by the end of the Golden Age, he had already established himself as a figure in the pantheon of jazz greats. And he became known as the coolest of the cool cats, not only in his playing but also in his behavior. When performing, he displayed a "drop dead" attitude. He'd blow his horn. Period. No mugging. No singing. No jokes. No dance steps. In fact, he sometimes contemptuously turned his back on his audience while taking solos. He kept real cool, man. But obviously there was a hot flame burning behind those ever-piercing eyes.

Miles Davis with Coleman Hawkins.

(OPPOSITE) *Miles Davis with Howard McGhee.*

(BELOW) *Miles Davis with Charlie Parker.*

INDEX

Numbers printed in bold type refer to illustrations.